CELTIC
BEASTS

Ex Libris

Courtney Davis

CELTIC BEASTS

Animal Motifs and Zoomorphic Design in Celtic Art

Text by Dennis O'Neill and Courtney Davis

BLANDFORD

A Blandford Book

First published in the UK 1999 by Blandford

A Cassell Imprint
Cassell plc
Wellington House
125 Strand
London WC2R 0BB
www.cassell.co.uk

Distributed in the United States by Sterling Publishing Co., Inc., 387 Park Avenue South, New York, NY 10016–8810

British Library Cataloguing-in-Publication Data
A catalogue entry for this title is available from the British Library

ISBN 0 7137 2727 6

Designed by Richard Carr
Printed and bound in Great Britain by Hillman Printers (Frome) Ltd, Somerset

Contents

Acknowledgements

Courtney Davis

I would like to thank my family and friends who have given me such great support through this book.

I would also like to thank Shining Bear and Trish Cardwell for their enthusiasm, and whose encouragement re-fired my imagination.

Thanks especially to Father Dennis O'Neill who has given me a greater insight to the images I produce and a better understanding of the worlds we live in.

Dennis O'Neill

This text is dedicated to my nieces and nephews, Elizabeth, Anthony, and Michael O'Neill, and Olivia, Huston and Wyatt Harris, of whom their forebears must be very proud.

This book is dedicated to the seen and unseen
worlds and the animal and natural kingdoms
who are so patient with us, and to the artists
of times past whose work still inspires and
amazes us today.

INTRODUCTION

THE BIBLE RELATES that Adam was given the authority to name all the animals. We are not told how the animals reacted to this, but, if they understood at all what was going on, they should have felt threatened. From the human perspective of that era, one who had the authority to name could also presume a certain amount of power and control over whatever had been identified. Such power was explicitly spelled out in Genesis 1:28: 'Rule over the fish in the ocean, the birds in the sky, and every animal on earth.' Calling by name often implied not so much the desire to be on intimate terms with the subjects, as an exercise of control over them, even if that control went no further than catching their attention. No wonder people eventually grew hesitant to call the God of Israel by name. One wouldn't want to appear presumptuous with a Deity!

In developing this aggressive, objectifying relationship with non-human reality, people not only began to

Cave drawing of Cernunnos found in Val Camonica, Italy, fourth–third century BCE

distance themselves from divinity but to place themselves in an antagonistic relationship with Mother Nature. Eventually, most people could no longer hear the animals speak.

Because the non-human inhabitants of this planet would probably find bewildering the need some humans have to compartmentalize creatures by boxing them into categories, the beasts treated in this book might even resent being labelled 'Celtic'. So it must be stated from the beginning that this book is a reflection not so much on the beasts themselves, as on what they meant to the Celts.

The Celts are the earliest identifiable northern European civilization. The Greek historian, Herodotus of Halicarnassus (c.490–425 BCE), in his second book *Histories*, points out that in his time the 'Keltoi' lived along the Danube River. Around 400 BCE, they crossed south of the Alps into the Po River valley. By then, they inhabited an area which extended as far east as western India, and

Painting of a mythical animal, who may be a magician, from the Lascaux caves, France

The bearded wine god Silenos in a feline form, from a bronze, fifth-century flagon

included Asia Minor, parts of the Balkans, present-day Austria, Germany, Switzerland, northern Italy, France, northern Spain, and Portugal. The unique culture, mythology, and art developed by these fierce warriors is considered the greatest achievement north of the Alps since the Ice Age. During the Roman period, just before the Celtic 'empire' began to wane, cities as wide apart as Ankara, Belgrade, Cologne, and Milan all spoke Celtic. The Romans usually called them Gauls, but Julius Caesar (100–44 BCE) wrote that the Gauls of his day referred to themselves as Celtae. When St Paul wrote to the Galatians, he was addressing Celts. By that time the Celts had already reached Britain and Ireland, where they subjugated the inhabitants and started to integrate cultural and religious systems which were to last for over half a millennium.

The Celts were a people deeply connected with creation. Animals were a constant part of Celtic life, both literally and symbolically. To this day in Ireland, if a bird happens to fly into the house, this can portend good luck. In the same way, if

Border from the Book of Durrow, *seventh century*

a frog hops into a house, it can mean that someone is about to die. Similarly, in the Scottish Highlands small birds are often considered harbingers of death.

The Celts not only relied on animals for their survival, but they respected them, learned from them, and honoured them. They decorated their jewellery, weapons, monuments, and, in the Christian period, their manuscripts, book covers, reliquaries, and chapels, with brilliant, intricate, elaborate zoomorphic designs.

In order to enter the world of Celtic beasts it is essential to set aside all linear thinking. To understand the role of animals in the ancient myths and in the lives of the saints, it is necessary to see them as more than either simple beasts or archetypal symbols. We are about to make a journey along a spiritual path, the origin of which can be traced to the earliest remaining evidence of human worship. Since archeologists have claimed that the bear is the oldest identifiable deity, we will begin with her.

There is a thread which forms a connecting link, running all the way

Detail from chancel arch at Taum, Galway, Ireland

back to the ancient Bear Mother and forward into Christian hagiography. That thread is shamanism, arguably the oldest spiritual discipline in the world. It is a complex of practices, magico-religious in character, whose primary focus is psycho-spiritual and psychosomatic healing. The word 'shaman' comes from Tungus, the ancient language of those who inhabit the Altai mountain region in Russian Siberia. Shamanic practice can also be found among the indigenous peoples of North, Central, and South America, the Arctic region, and Australia. The root word *s'aman* can be translated 'to burn up' or 'to set on fire', referring to a shaman's ability to work with the energy of heat. Shamanism was practised by the Celts and seems to have been an aspect of their druidic training which was ultimately blended into the spiritual discipline of the Celtic church. Several authors have sought antecedents for druidism among ancient shamans, perhaps even the Altaic ones, arguing that this connection opens up a vista of 20,000 years. We can sense how connected the Celtic saints were with their ancient shamanic forebears when we recall that the ability to handle either

fire or hot coals was a skill frequently demonstrated by these saints.

In the archaic past of human evolution, before any of the great religions came into being, shamans were the first to emerge as the mediators of the sacred for their people. The great twentieth-century anthropologist Mircea Eliade defined shamanism primarily as a technique of ecstasy. In situations where the information required for healing or survival was unobtainable, shamans would put themselves into an altered state of consciousness, during which the soul would leave the body and make a journey. Presuming that we, the living inhabitants of Earth, are denizens of the shamanic Middleworld, the shamans' souls would either ascend to the Upperworld or descend to the Lowerworld. There they would meet and confer with their 'spirit guides' – either human or animal – who would help them either to obtain the information they sought, or otherwise to achieve their journey's purpose. In the altered state of consciousness, which is an essential component of shamanic experience, many sorts of animals are apt to appear. Far from being

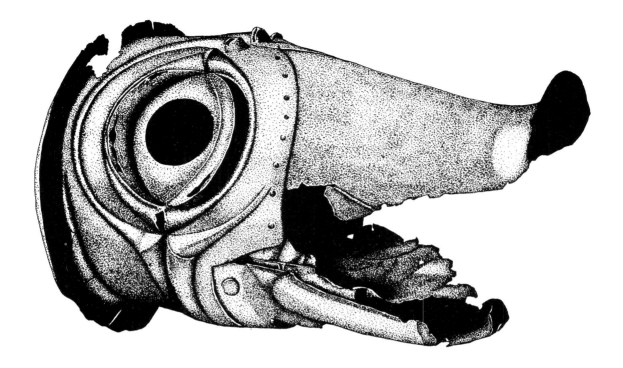

Bronze carynx head representing a boar, first century CE

subject to humankind, they serve rather as helpers and spiritual guides. In the shamanic Otherworld animals can talk, move about like humans, jest, warn, and shapeshift. In this world animals frequently function as teachers from whom humans learn. Since the human 'spirit guides' are recognizable people who actually lived on Earth earlier in history, it is possible that the animal spirit guides are even older and come from a period in history which precedes the emergence of the human race. They may literally be our pre-human relatives.

As human history unfolded, shamans, and other mediators between this world and the spirit world, may have realized that certain animals appeared to be consistently associated with specific aspects of life. Thus pigs became connected with the Underworld, and salmon and eels with wisdom. This may be why certain animals were deified at first, and later came to be associated with specific divinities. Sometimes, through the language of Christian iconographic symbolism, the divinized animal reappeared after having shapeshifted into the constant companion, or

the metaphoric symbol, of the saint. This is how St Anthony the Abbot acquired his pig companion and became patron of gravediggers.

A more extended example of this can be seen in the tenth-century Byzantine missionaries in Kiev, who blended the fourth-century bishop and martyr St Blaise (Vlasios) of Sebaste with the ancient god Volos who had been worshipped both as lord of wild animals (especially bears), cattle and wealth, and as a guardian of the entrance to the Underworld. As part of this syncretism, they incorporated into the legend of 'St Vlas' an episode where he hid in a cave and became a protector of the forest animals. When devotion to St Blaise was carried to Europe, he was also blended with the Celtic deity Cernunnos – likewise a lord of the forest animals and guardian of the entrance to the Underworld. The chthonic function of these old gods was blended into Christian experience when chapels to St Blaise were erected in places which had previously been considered entrances to the Underworld by the earlier Celtic inhabitants. To stress the point further, the feast of St Blaise was linked with those of St Brigid

Deer ornament from an iron scabbard, second century BCE

Our departed ancestors have preceded us into the Otherworld, as have our shamanic forbears, the old divinities, and the saints. They live on in memory and in eternity. What remains constant from age to age is Mother Earth and her wide variety of non-human inhabitants. If, through artistic symbolism, the goddess Artemis and the god Cernunnos could continue to be identified because of their stag companions, so could the saints Cadoc, Teilo, Hurbert, Eustace and many others who followed. Since their stags are never named, we are allowed to wonder whether they might not be the same stag reappearing again and again, whose true home is the shamanic Otherworld. If we can come to understand this Otherworld stag better, we might be better able to appreciate the splendour of a living stag. Glancing through a Celtic lens we might begin to gain deeper insight into all kinds of beasts. This book is intended to be such a lens.

Stag from the Gündestrup cauldron, first century CE

and Candlemas, which in Rome absorbed the old pagan festival of Lupercalia – with St Brigid, our Lady of Candlemas, and St Blaise replacing Proserpina/ Persephone, Ceres/Demeter and Pluto/Hades. Then this triduum of feasts absorbed the ancient Celtic festival of Imbolc, another celebration of spring's return from the Underworld. In old representations, both eastern and western, St Blaise was still sometimes shown accompanied by his animals as well as holding the candles which connected him with Imbolc.

There is another tale of St Blaise, in which he orders a wolf to return a stolen pig to the woman from whom he stole it. In the various Gaelic tongues the word for wolf is derived from 'Blaise'. For example, the Breton word *blez* means 'wolf'. In this tale the pig can be seen to represent the Underworld, and it is possible that the wolf stealing the pig represents Hades stealing Persephone, who, like the pig returned to the woman, is eventually returned to her mother Demeter.

Finally, of course, the Old English word *blaze* means 'to burn brightly', which relates the name Blaise to the root meaning of the word 'shaman'.

THE BEAR - THE OLDEST DEITY

THE BEAR IS no longer indigenous to the British Isles, nor to Ireland, and it does not appear in old Celtic stories. We begin with the bear, because its veneration is so ancient. The Celts received it from their European Stone Age ancestors in the form of the goddess Brigid. Stone figures of bears from the pagan Celtic period were found in 1840 during the rebuilding of Ireland's Armagh Cathedral. At Meigle in Perthshire, Scotland, an old Pictish centre, there are several carved crosses, and other inscribed stone monuments, displaying Pictish designs. Among these is an eighth-century

carving of a bear. Another Pictish carving depicting a fearsome bear can be seen on one of the slabs at St Vigeans, Angus, Scotland. The bear also appears in illuminated manuscripts prepared by Celtic monks. The earliest ancestors of those ursine products of skilled monastic whimsy can be found on the walls of caves.

There are reasons for suggesting that the early wall paintings depicting bears were done by shamans. The deliberate distortions of detail on some animals –

The Great Bear

additional legs or incredibly large horns – suggest that they may have been painted in an altered state of consciousness. Also, they seem to have been painted using a form of oral spray painting rather than by brush; spitting was a shamanic way of projecting oneself onto the wall. It has been suggested that Chauvet's cave, discovered by Jean-Marie Chauvet near Avignon, France, in 1994, was a sort of Paleolithic cathedral, for it even contained an 'altar' – a bear's skull, carefully perched on a rock.

This is not the first time such reverently placed bear skulls have been discovered in caves. Many archeologists have concluded that, by the Paleolithic period, humans were capable of spiritual insight and had begun to use religious symbolism. It is believed that humans and bears were associated in a way that suggested a concept either of an afterlife, or reincarnation, or both. This association was most likely made because humans were able to observe the way bears hibernated, entering into a death-like state and then returning to life with the spring. It seems that bears were considered to be guides of the Underworld, who each year would track down spring during hibernation and bring it back. As hunters, the Cro-Magnon admired the bears' great strength; as parents, they admired the mother bears' ferocity in protecting and nurturing their cubs. They also appreciated the way that the flesh on the bear kept it alive until spring's return, and the way that the fur kept it warm.

Archeologists have concluded that the Bear Mother is the oldest identifiable deity, and the genealogy of several ancient goddesses can be traced back to the Bear Mother. In 1832 a statue of Dea Artio, a Helvetian-Celtic lunar bear goddess, was exhumed from beneath the streets of Berne, ('She Bear'), Switzerland. The Celts also called her by the shortened name of Art. A similar goddess worshipped at Cologne, Germany, became the Schwabian goddess Ursel, or Hörsel, who, in the Middle Ages, shapeshifted and reappeared as St Ursula. The names Brigid, and the Scandinavian Birgit, are both derived from the Indo-European root word for 'bear'. Brigid was the most beloved of the pan-Celtic goddesses. It is recorded of St Brigid of Kildare, in her earliest known biography, *Life of St Brigid the Virgin* written by Cogitosus ua hÁeda in the seventh century, that not only was she fond of beer, but that she miraculously transformed vats of water into beer. Like the Bear Mother, the goddess

Brigid was considered a mother goddess (and virgin as well), a healer, an Underworld divinity, both solar and lunar, and the 'Bride' of spring. The name Brigid is so ancient and universal in root, that it can also be traced back to the Sanskrit feminine adjective *brhati*, which was used as a divine epithet meaning 'great,' 'lofty,' 'exalted,' and 'brightly shining'.

In addition to Dea Artio, the Celtic goddess Andarta ('Strong Bear') was worshipped throughout Gaul. The name of the Greek grain goddess, Demeter (Ceres in Rome), literally translates as 'the grain of the bear mother', or 'barley mother', thus revealing her direct descent from the Bear Mother. Barley ('bear's grain') is incubated underground to make beer, and this link hints further that Demeter, Ceres, and Brigid are either all cousins, or the same goddess in different manifestations. Barley, in Italian is *orzo*, and in French it is *orge*, revealing that the connection between bear and barley continues in some of the romance languages. A further ursine goddess even more widely known and venerated throughout the Mediterranean world was Artemis.

The Celts seem to have arrived in Britain and Ireland in waves. The first wave of invaders was very likely the Fir Bolg, or Belgae, who seem to have arrived, accompanied by the Dunnonii and the Gauls, possibly in the fifth century BCE. Next there was an invasion from northern Europe. These were likely the Tuatha de Danaan – the people of the goddess Danu, an old European mother goddess, after whom the Don, Dnieper, and Danube rivers are named. Then came the Gaels, the 'sons of Mil', invading from the south, possibly via Spain.

One Celtic group, the Brigantes, settled both in Wexford and in the Yorkshire area, occupying an extensive territory, which reached from the North Sea to the Irish Sea. Under the name Brigantia (Britannia), they claimed Brigid as their primary divinity, the goddess from whom the tribe's name is derived. The names of cities throughout Europe proclaim that she was already venerated there before being brought to Britain and Ireland. Among them are Bragança (Portugal), Bregenz (western Austria), Briançon (France), Corunna (on the northwest coast of Spain, originally called Brigantia), and Nemetobriga (northern Spanish Galicia, translating as 'Brigid's Sacred Grove'). Brigeto, in Illyricum (former Yugoslavia), was the location of one of her earliest shrines. The Romans knew her as the

The Bear Mother

Alpine protectress of travellers and claimed that she had a sky-god consort named Poeninus. The Italian Apennine and the British Pennine mountains bear his name. In the Middle Ages, St Brigid of Kildare (d. 525 CE) was considered a patron saint of travellers and pilgrims. To this day, in northwest Italy, celestial protection for travellers is sought under the combined patronage of the sixth-century Celtic saints Brigid and Ursus ('Bear') of Aosta, who share the same feast of 1 February. The city of Ivrea once had a church dedicated to them. Together they were the city's patrons, both honoured as bringers of good weather.

It is particularly in her role as the harbinger of spring that Brigid shows her ursine quality. Her festival of Imbolc falls on 1 February, the vigil of the day which, throughout Europe and America is still honored as an auspicious time when many festivals and celebrations focus on the end of hibernation. In parts of Eastern Europe, Candlemas is still called 'Bear Day' because it falls on the date which is traditionally assigned as the end of hibernation. In France and several other parts of Europe, one of the most enduring mythological figures to appear among those costumed for pre-Lenten celebrations is the 'Candlemas Bear'. Elsewhere, the bear has been shrunk and domesticated into the Irish hedgehog and the American groundhog. In Scotland, the ancient serpent cult was apparently so strong that she remained the one to end hibernation and herald the spring. There and in the Hebrides Brigid and the serpent were invoked together, as though the two were one.

The serpent

*Pictish symbol stone
fourth–fifth century CE*

THERE IS PLENTY of evidence in Ireland and Scotland that an ancient serpent cult once flourished there. The megalithic tumulus at New Grange, Ireland, shows a curled serpentine monument. Crude serpent carvings adorn pyramidal stones overlooking the plains of Dundalk, County Louth, Ireland. Serpent worship was common in Argyll, Scotland, which was Irish by contiguity and racial descent. There is also a great serpent mound near Inverary, and a mound on the Clyde River is the remains of an ancient serpent earthwork. At the entrance of a chambered tomb (*c.* 3000 BCE) at Knockmany, County Tyrone, is carved an image of the goddess Aine-as-hag, who spouts serpentine forms from her mouth. A carved sandstone image of a three-eyed, open-mouthed serpent was also found at Knowth, County Meath, and dates from 2500 BCE. At Pool, on Sanday in the Orkneys, sixth-century structure alterations required the reuse of two stones upon which were carved 'proto-symbols' from a much earlier period. Among them is a serpent head. On a wall in King's Cove Cave on Arran can be found an interlacing snake design, which may have been carved around 700 CE. The ram-headed serpent appears frequently in pre-Christian Celtic and Scandinavian art. A famous example can be seen in the left hand of the shamanic Cernunnos figure portrayed on the Gündestrup cauldron of the first or second century BCE, discovered in a Danish peat bog. In Pictish symbolism the ram-headed serpent's equivalent is bull-headed.

Like the bear, the serpent was a major religious symbol long before the Celts emerged as a distinct people. Not only does the serpent also hibernate during winter and reappear with the coming of spring, but it also emerges from its own sloughed-off skin, which led people to believe that it had the power of self-renewal. The moon also appeared to have the same power, because of its waxing and waning, and so the serpent often came to be associated with lunar deities. It became the quintessential symbol of life, fertility, rejuvenation, regeneration, and immortality. While clearly also a solar phallic symbol in most ancient cultures, before patriarchal religion displaced them, the serpent was primarily a symbol, or an adornment, of the Great Goddess, representing her and mediating her relationship with human culture.

Because of the powerful hold she had on the minds and hearts of humans, the serpent was demonized in the Bible in the book of Genesis. The biblical narration hints at the nature of this hold when it says 'the serpent was the most subtle of all the wild beasts...' Subtle in this sense means clever, crafty, wily, cunning, keen, penetrating, discriminating, skillful, abstruse, not easy to understand, and some of these attributes would eventually be considered as characterizing Divine Wisdom. The Semitic word 'Hawwah' (in English the biblical Eve), not only means 'mother of all the living', but also 'serpent' in several Semitic languages. It has been theorized that in the more ancient stories from which Genesis evolved, the original three characters in Paradise were God, Adam (meaning 'man' in Hebrew) and a serpent deity – who was probably the original one to be expelled from Paradise. Later in history, even the monotheistic Moses would use a bronze serpent as a healing icon. Until destroyed by King Hezekiah of Judah (716–687 BCE), it was preserved for over 500 years, and displayed as a revered relic in the Jerusalem temple, where people offered sacrifices to it.

Despite its demonization, the serpent's ancient attributes were so deeply rooted in people's collective consciousness that Jesus told his disciples to 'be as wise as a serpent' (Matthew 10:16). Thus, even in Christ's own terminology, the serpent represented wisdom; and in many ancient systems of myth, symbol, and thought, wisdom was associated with Creation. In Proverbs 8:27–31 it is claimed that

wisdom was 'by God's side, a master craftswoman' when Creation came into being.

The serpent also appears on Scotland's Pictish sculptures. It was apparently one of their most powerful symbols. It was also one of their most complex, for it had many meanings. In addition to those already mentioned, the zigzagging serpent represented the great, meandering rivers. Nicholas Mann has pointed out that the zigzag is the earliest Egyptian hieroglyph for flowing water, and that many British rivers were named after different words for serpents, among them the Wye, Wyle, Esk, Adur, Exe, and Axe. Likewise, throughout Ireland there are bodies of water whose names include variations on the word *piastra* ('serpent').

Cernunnos holding a torc and a serpent, adapted from the first century CE Gündestrup Cauldron

When coiled with its tail in its mouth, the serpent symbolized infinitude, omnipotence, and omniscience. In a spiral, it symbolized the cycles of evolution and reincarnation. The serpent was a challenge to dualistic thinking. When depicted crawling, it symbolized evil; but an erect serpent represented good. It signified both female and male, joy and tragedy, life and death, loving and hating, and always new beginnings.

This last aspect is apparent in the serpent's connection with the feast of St Brigid (Bride in Scotland and the Hebrides). During the later portion of the nineteenth century, the folklorist Alexander Carmichael devoted over 60 years to researching and recording Scottish and Hebridean lore and texts. Among the material he preserved can be found several variations of the following propitiatory hymn:

Early on Bride's morn,
The serpent shall come from the hole,
I will not molest the serpent,
Nor will the serpent molest me.

Anne Ross, *The Folklore of the Scottish Highlands* (1976) p. 120

The serpent was originally worshipped in Scotland and the Hebrides as a hibernating animal who appeared as the Bride of spring and who brought protection from evil. On the same day, a strange custom took place which seemed to contradict serpent worship – a ritual pounding of the serpent in effigy. An old woman would take a piece of peat from the fire and place it in her stocking, thus forming a crude serpent shape. Then she laid it on the threshold of the house and would pound it with the tongs while saying:

This is the Day of Bride,
The queen will come from the mound,
I will not touch the queen,
Nor will the queen touch me.

Anne Ross, *The Folklore of the Scottish Highlands* (1976) p. 130

Here Bride is both serpent and queen and, as in the previous text, seems to be treated as though she were not entirely beneficent. Recalling that in addition to being the Bride of Spring, Brigid was also a goddess of wisdom and of the rivers, it is apparent that she was connected with the serpent in several ways.

The combination of serpent and Z symbol on Pictish sculpture seems to have represented an initiatory process in which the shaman, druid, or bard learned how to expand their own

Detail from the twelfth-century Irish Cross of Cong

contracted energy so that it could flow through the body's energy centres, thus simultaneously cleansing and charging the system. In the Indian tantric process of Kundalini Yoga, the dormant goddess Kundalini ('coiled up'), called Shakti by the Shivite sect, symbolizes the inner female soul, coiled like a serpent in the pelvis. An initiate can learn to move the body's energy in such a way that it uncoils up the spine from its base, ascending towards the head, through the seven perception centres called the chakras, finally reaching the crown and exploding into pure consciousness, bringing the gifts of enlightenment and wisdom. This energy rush creates a sort of interior feminine orgasm into consciousness which parallels the exterior masculine orgasm. When serpents appear in twins they represent both this dual orgasm and the complementarity and balance of female and male energies which we all have – another manifestation of the relationship between wisdom and creation. They were a Celtic yin and yang.

Under the shadow of the Genesis curse, the serpent continued to be demonized by Christians. A cluster of stories emerged whose common theme was the attempt by several saints to banish it or destroy it. There is no word for dragon or serpent in early Irish, except when borrowed from British or Latin tradition (Caitlin Matthews, *Arthur and the Sovereignty of Britain,* Arkana, New York, 1989, p. 47). This may mean that there were indeed no serpents either. Even though Solinus wrote in the second century that there were no serpents in Ireland, St Patrick is widely credited with having driven them out three centuries later. Another legend has the later St Kevin seeing to the destruction of the last Irish serpent when he let his dog Lupus (Latin for 'wolf') kill it. He then threw the

Detail from the Book of Kells, *eighth–ninth century*

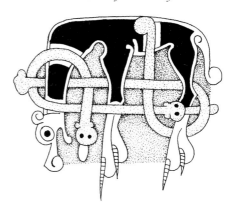

*Left: Thor holding his hammer and
hauling in line after the World Serpent
has taken his x-head bait. Adapted from
a stone carving, ninth–tenth century*

creature into the lake at Glendalough, which is why it is named Lochnapiast ('Lake of the Serpent'). St Cado is said to have driven the serpents out of Brittany, while saints David and Iltud rendered the same service to Wales.

The manifest presence of the serpent in Christian Celtic art is proof of the saints' failure to neutralize its appeal. After 664 CE, when the Synod of Whitby decided that Roman Church customs would replace Celtic, there was a deliberate attempt to suppress any Christianized druidic knowledge and traditions. Nicholas Mann claims that the reality of this threat was perceived by the druids, and rather than risk the utter sublimation of the Ancient Living Tradition into the Inner Worlds, they attempted to encode their knowledge, literally their consciousness, into the Symbol Stones of Alba (Nicholas R. Mann, *The Keltic Power Symbols*, p. 20).

Thus in Scotland, while on the one hand St Columba is said to have driven off the mysterious water beast of Loch Ness with a blessing, and in like manner to have rendered the snakes of Iona harmless, on the other hand some of his monastic descendants were among those who sculpted snake bosses on to St Martin's cross on Iona, the great stone cross at Kildalton on the Isle of Islay, and the Nigg Cross slab in Ross in the eighth century, as well as into the intricate designs on the cross slab at Meigle in Perthshire and others at Aberlamno at Glamis and St Vigeans in Angus.

When the Vikings and the Danes invaded the Celtic countries, they brought with them their own serpent lore. There are ancient accounts of the god Thor slaying the World Serpent. This theme was depicted on a stone inside the Gosforth Church in Cumbria, a tenth-century panel which was probably originally part of a Christian cross. It was also carved on a stone discovered at Repton in Derbyshire. The World Serpent was said to coil around the base of a great ash tree called Yggdrasil, beneath which the Norse pantheon gathered when the time came to determine the fate of gods and humans. The eagle was at its top, while at the base of the tree was Mimir's Spring (*memor* is Latin for 'mindfulness') which was considered the fountain of all wit and wisdom, in whose liquid depths even the future was said to be clearly mirrored. Yggdrasil served as a shamanic symbol, whose function was similar to the druidic oak. Trees whose roots extended deep into the earth and whose branches reached to the skies represented the options shamans had to journey either to the Underworld or to the Upperworld. The denizens of these places were either helpful, tricky, or morally neutral, but not evil. From its Underworld home, the serpent was considered a powerful dispenser of blessing and rejuvenation.

THE OLDEST ANIMALS

WHEN THE CELTS spoke about 'oldest animals', they were not concerned about which beasts emerged earlier than others in evolutionary order, or which creatures were believed to have had special significance from the earlier periods in Celtic history. 'Oldest' meant rather that greater power and wisdom were attributed to those beasts who were known to have longer life spans. Since these animals had more time than others to observe life and were unhampered by human prejudices, they were thought to have acquired great wisdom. The Celts trusted that their Otherworld counterparts would probably be the more helpful creatures to serve as guides and mentors in various areas of need. Even though the Otherworld had its own rules, a careful observation of animal behaviour in this world could give clues about what might be expected of the Otherworld beasts.

A curious European custom which developed before the beginning of the Middle Ages was the calculating of dates by multiplying by three the number of years traditionally ascribed to various living creatures. Examples which have survived in Greek, Latin, Italian, Spanish, Portuguese, Breton, German, Welsh, Scottish, and Irish, reveal the approximate life spans people attributed to various beasts, ordering them sequentially according to relative length. While some beasts regularly appear in these listings, very few lists are identical. A Celtic example can be found in the fifth-century *Book of Lismore*, a portion of which reads:

> Three lifetimes of the hound for the horse,
> Three lifetimes of the horse for the human being,
> Three lifetimes of the human being, the stag,
> Three lifetimes of the stag for the ousel,
> Three lifetimes of the ousel for the eagle,
> Three lifetimes of the eagle for the salmon...

Caitlín and John Matthews, *The Encyclopaedia of Celtic Wisdom*, p. 65

Another example can be found in the *Book of Ballymote*, which lists the animals in the sequence of hound, horse, human being, deer and salmon.

In addition to these lists, which are simply comparative life spans of certain animals, a group of stories emerged in Ireland in which several long-lived creatures have a definite function. They are described as survivors of the Great Flood, who undergo many trials as they pursue their mission of carrying forward the early traditions of the race. The oldest of these stories is found in the twelfth-century edition of the *Book of the Dun Cow*, and concerns Tuan mac Carell, an old Donegal warrior who was reputed to know the history of all the races who ever inhabited Ireland. When St Finnian established his monastery at Moville around the year 540 CE, and heard about Tuan's reputation, he went to him, requesting that he come and recount his tales to the monastic community. When the crusty old unbeliever refused and shut the door in Finnian's face, the abbot used a typically Celtic method of shaming him into doing what he wanted. He began a hunger-strike. Meanwhile, Tuan went to sleep and, during the night, transformed into a venerable cleric. It was in this form that he greeted Finnian in the morning and, after they both had said their prayers, agreed to come and narrate what turned out to be the story of the five successive invasions of Ireland – those of Partholan, Nemedh, the Fir Bolg, the Tuatha de Danaan, and the Milesians. Tuan claimed personally to have witnessed all these events, and he explained how this was possible. When he had reached a great old age, he fell asleep one night and woke up a young stag. When the stag became ancient, it fell asleep and woke up a young boar, which in old age became a hawk, which in turn became a salmon. When the ancient salmon was caught and eaten by Tuan's mother, Tuan was conceived and born. He remembered everything he experienced under these transformations, thus increasing his wisdom during each lifetime. So historical memory was preserved by Tuan during his animal phases, while he continued living through a process of transmigration, which included the aspects of metamorphosis (change of form), metempsychosis (passing from one body to another after death), and reincarnation (being born again). If Tuan ever actually existed, the one way he could have experienced this combination of shapeshifting and acquiring ancient wisdom during one lifetime would have been through having the ability to make shamanic journeys.

According to a Welsh tale about the divine Gwydion, son of Don (the goddess Danu), and his brother Gilvaethwy, they are turned by their uncle Math, Lord of Gwynedd, into deer, then swine, and then wolves, before becoming themselves again. In another tale, the swineherds Rucht and Rucne become birds, wolves, fish, worms and finally bulls – in this latter form they kill one another and become spirits. In another tale, the four children of the Danaan divinity Lir are turned into white swans. In yet another, the heroine Étain is turned into a butterfly before being reborn as herself.

These tales probably reveal vestiges of initiation processes. It took twenty years for a druid or a bard to be trained fully. During those years, each initiate would have had to learn every aspect of the history, traditions, and religious observances of the race. They would have learned how to make shamanic journeys for the double purpose of obtaining healing knowledge and of recovering other vital information, which had somehow been lost to history and tradition.

Adapted from the Book of Kells, *eighth–ninth century*

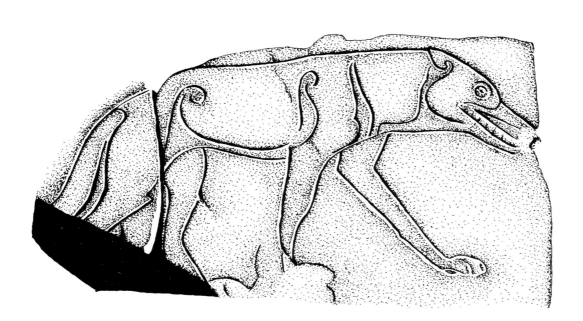

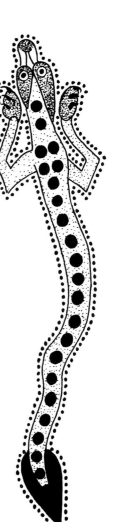

The great sixth-century Welsh bard, Taliesin, was the inheritor of a British shamanic tradition which seems to have been still flourishing in his day. The amazing tale of his birth is probably laden with details which reflect aspects of his own bardic initiation. According to the tale, when the boy Gwion Bach accidentally swallowed three drops from the goddess Ceridwen's cauldron, he received her gifts of inspiration and wisdom. Since she had intended the brew for her son Afagddu, she became enraged and began to pursue Gwion. In order to escape, he turned into a hare. Whereupon she turned into a black greyhound. He became a fish and she pursued him as an otter. He became a bird and she turned into a hawk. He then turned into a grain of wheat hiding in a winnowed heap. She became a hen and swallowed him. He quickened in her womb, and nine months later she gave birth to the child who would be given the name Taliesin, which means 'radiant brow'. In one of his own poems, the adult Taliesin would claim to have been a buck, a wild sow, a speckled cat, and a goat during his life.

The Irish tale called 'The Frenzy of Suibhne' came into its present form around 1200 CE. It tells how King Suibhne (Sweeney) of Dal Araidhe in Northern Ireland went mad during the battle of Magh Rath in 837 CE, how he subsequently sprouted feathers and flew like a

Above: Seventh-century stone carving of a wolf

Right: Serpent from the Book of Kells, *eighth–ninth century*

bird, and how he rode on a fawn, leading a herd of stags like a regular Lord of the Forest. The specific reason for the madness was a curse put on the king by St Ronan, who had tried to halt the battle, but ended up losing one of his clerics to Suibhne himself, who thrust a javelin into him. The riding of a stag also figures in an earlier tale, when Suibhne's counterpart, Myrddin Lailoken, does so during his own madness after the Battle of Arthuret in 573 CE. Both Suibhne and Myrddin were clearly in an altered state of consciousness during these phases.

An example of the way the oldest animals give assistance can be found in the Welsh saga of 'Culwch and Olwen', in which the blackbird, stag, eagle, and salmon are consulted concerning the whereabouts of the lost divine child Mabon, who is eventually found and rescued by Arthur's warriors with the assistance of various animals.

Shapeshifting

HILE MOST PEOPLE would respond to the notion of literal shape-shifting with disbelief or fear, we see examples of the phenomenon so frequently that we take it for granted. Any good actor is a shapeshifter. So are Christian clergy when they preside in sanctuaries and are understood to stand in the place of Christ and mediate his presence in word and sacrament. In fact, all theatre can find its origin in ancient public worship.

Painting of a sorcerer from a cave at Les Trois Frères in the French Pyrennees

The two main reasons for shapeshifting are either to mediate the presence of another being or to protect oneself in threatening situations. According to legend, from our primordial beginnings when life was still raw and we knew no separation between instinct and intellect or between body and spirit, humans had an intimate, inspired relationship with the other creatures of this planet. Humans and animals understood each other well enough to be able to assume each others' roles when necessary with the same skill used today by good actors and actresses. When, later in history, humans and animals took the evolutionary paths which drew them away from each others, the ability to assume each others' roles began to disappear. Metamorphosis then became a secret skill, belonging primarily to the domain of shamans, sorcerers, and saints.

One aspect of the human ability to shapeshift which survived into a later period of history was during the heat of battle. The Norse were famous for the ferocious, frenzied state into which they could work themselves before entering battle. As one part of the process, they would put on bearskin shirts to aid their shapeshifting into beings with the assumed, stature, gait, and ferocity of bears. For this reason, they were called *Berserkers* (from the Old Norse words *ber* ['bear'] and *sark* ['shirt']). The ceremonial troops of the British Army still wear bearskins albeit as a rather impractical sort of headdress. Likewise, the legendary Irish warrior and solar hero, Cuchulain, son of the god Lugh, exhibited the 'hero's light', a flaming aura, around his head when he entered the state of battle frenzy. He is said to have been able to perform a 'salmon's leap', which is a solar image and refers to his being able to cover great distances or leap to remarkable heights effortlessly. He seemed to be able to revolve in his skin and fight in every direction at once. His forehead swelled, and a fiery shaft rose from his crown. His blood boiled, and his hair stood on end with drops of blood at the tips of every strand.

Aurae of a different kind could be seen around the heads of many saints. Witnesses occasionally saw both Brigid and Columba with bright radiance around their heads and even with shafts of light rising from the crown of their heads towards the sky. To this day, the addition of a halo to any portrait is a universally recognizable symbol of holiness in this life.

Image from a sixth-century die for making helmet plates, depicting a Viking Berserker warrior. In the fury of battle they were able to shapeshift into bears or wolves

Two bird-headed men carved on to the seventh-century Papil Stone, Shetland

When shamans undertake the journey to the Otherworld, the power animals they meet on the other side serve as their guides. As shamans become acquainted with their particular guides, they can then use masks, or skulls, hides, pelts or other actual parts of these beasts to facilitate their identification with them as they enter into a trance-like state. During such journeys, witnesses will sometimes see shamans take on the characteristics of their power animals and begin, either consciously or unconsciously, to imitate their sounds and actions. The stag-antlered and pelted painting of a sorcerer with a bear's fore-paws, and a bison-headed musician, that were depicted sometime between 13,000–9,000 BCE on the cave wall at Les Trois Frères deep under the Pyrenees, reveal that such shamanic practices already existed in the Old Stone Age. Similarly, the two bird-headed men supporting a human head between their beaks, carved beneath a lion and a Christian cross on the Papil Stone in Burra, Shetland, in the late seventh century, hint that a rich shamanic tradition lasted among the Picts well into the Christian era. Such practices have been continued throughout history in several parts of the world, and have been resumed in many others at the end of the twentieth century.

The other main reason to shapeshift is for self-preservation. Chameleons are well known for their ability to change colours in order to blend into their environment. They are not the only beasts able to make this adjustment. Colourshifting creatures can be found in many varieties, both on land and in the sea.

In many Celtic legends, the ability to shapeshift into various beasts was ascribed to divinities, heroes, or heroines. While it is often a shamanic or ecstatic experience that is being described, sometimes it is clear that a literal shapeshifting is meant. Even some of the Christian saints underwent such metamorphoses. The most famous example is St Patrick. According to Muirchú moccu Machteni's eighth-century *Life of St Patrick*, when Patrick realized that he and his disciples were in danger of being attacked by King Laoghaire of Tara, he blessed them at the beginning of a journey. While the king and his men were waiting to ambush the eight men and boy, all Laoghaire saw passing through that day were eight deer and a fawn.

St Ronan, the abbot who cursed Suibhne, was also supposedly a shapeshifter. Jean Markale quotes hagiographer Albert Le Grand, who wrote of him:

> ...it was claimed that he was a sorcerer and necromancer, that he was like the ancient lycanthropes (werewolves) which, by means of magic and diabolical art, transformed themselves into wild animals, and roamed the groves, causing a thousand evils in the country...

Jean Markale, *Merlin*, p. 165

The reference here to werewolves is important. *Were* is said to derive from the German *wer*, a cognate of the Latin *vir*, which simply means 'man'. Werewolf literally means 'man/wolf'. Many other kinds of 'were-animals' are mentioned in world lore. Writing in 1183, Giraldus Cambrensis recorded that, only three years before, a priest travelling from Ulster to Meath was resting for the night on the Meath border with a young lad companion when they were stunned by the approach of a friendly talking wolf. This wolf explained that, because of a curse put on the town of Ossory by St Natalis, a sixth-century abbot who was a fellow-worker with St Columba, every seven years a man and woman had to venture into the wilderness, where they would be turned into wolves. If they survived for seven years, they could return to human shape, and another couple would take their place. Giraldus claimed to have been appraised of this matter by the Bishop of Meath himself, who asked him to adjudicate in an Episcopal review of the case. Such behaviour might have been barely tolerable in saints (with their ability to turn themselves or others into wolves, they would have been able to subdue most potential opponents anyway!) but, when ascribed to other kinds of people, it sounds pretty scary. According to the biblical book of Daniel 4:30, because of a prophecy uttered against him King Nebuchadnezzar of Babylon ended up 'driven from human society and fed on grass like oxen, and was drenched by the dew of heaven; his hair grew as long as eagles' feathers, and his nails became like birds' claws.' He seems to have lost his mind.

Most lesbian, gay, bisexual, or transgendered people know all about 'passing', since many have passed as heterosexuals for much or all of their lives. It is important to realize that it takes a great deal of genuine understanding of what other people think, how they feel, and how they behave before anyone can convincingly pass as one of their number. This means – theoretically at least – that people of same-sex inclination (homosexual) or opposite sex identity (transgendered) would normally have a well-developed capacity for empathy and compassion. Among several Native American tribes, such people were thought to constitute a third gender and were among the most famous shamans, healers, and marriage counsellors. They were thought to be more self-contained than heterosexuals because they could empathize with the sensibilities of both women and men. In fact several writers have pointed out that many shamans throughout the world are either androgynous or bi-sexual.

Another reason the Celts costumed as animals was to protect themselves from the winter – the season of chaos and dismemberment. Furs, hides, and pelts were not only worn for warmth. Winter was a frightening time of year when most of nature seemed to die, crops would not grow, and only salted meat and the reserves from the previous harvest were available for sustenance. People could starve or freeze to death during winter. It was not a good season for animals either, for they too had a harder time foraging for food and were more susceptible to disease than at other times of the year. The powers of blight were beginning their ascendancy. Since the powers of growth were in danger and in eclipse, people thought it necessary to assist them. The Celts believed that, during the winter, the sun, in full strength, was sojourning in the Otherworld. The Irish St Virgilius (in Irish 'Fearghal'), Bishop of Salzburg (d. 784 CE), was once attacked by St Boniface of Crediton for teaching that there is another one below this earth, with its own sun and moon, where elves and gnomes lived. Since this Underworld had its own sun, it had no need of ours, so, by various means, people tried to trick the warm sun into returning. The Samhain (Halloween) bonfire was the main magical aid to entice the sun back. In addition to this, disguising in the shaggy hides of various beasts or costuming as denizens of the Otherworld was carried out as a way of 'containing' the winter season. By shapeshifting in this way, people held up a mirror to the Otherworld in order to trick the sun into returning to this side. To this day, Halloween and Mardi Gras are the two times of year in which many Westerners routinely dress up in costumes.

The shapeshifter

The cow and the bull

IN THE YEAR 598 CE the Chief Bard of Ireland, Senchan Torpeist, called a meeting of bards and storytellers to see if together they could remember the great epic poem, the *Taín Bó Cuailgnè* ('The Cattle Raid of Cooley'). Since they found they could only piece together fragments, Senchan sent forth two young poets who were to seek out an ancient book which was said to contain the entire text and which had been apparently given away in exchange for a copy of St Isidore of Seville's *Culmen*. On their way, they reached Magh Aei in Roscommon, site of the tomb of Fergus Mac Roy (an Anglicization of *Ro-ech* meaning 'Great Horse'), an Ulster King who had been friendly to Cuchulainn. One of the poets began to recite a poem of his own and was immediately enveloped in a thick fog in which Mac Roy himself appeared and recited the entire *Taín Bó Cualingè* over a period of three days and nights.

This story is an example of the way a bard could use poetic recitation as a means of entering a shamanic trance, which led to the meeting of an Otherworld figure who could help the shaman to retrieve important lost knowledge. In a Christianized version of the same story, it was the Irish saints who, earlier that century, gathered at Mac Roy's tomb on the same quest. He appeared to St Ciaran of Clonmacnois (d. 556 CE), who recorded the entire epic on vellum made from the hide of his favourite dun cow. The book which was thereafter constructed came to be known as the *Book of the Dun Cow*, which is the oldest remaining Irish manuscript in which mythological tales are recorded. The present copy was made by a scribe named Maelmuiri, who was killed by robbers at Clonmacnois in 1106. This story has some interesting aspects. It shows Christian monks recognizing the Otherworld as a source of knowledge unobtainable by any other method. In an earlier generation, St Patrick likewise is said to have

The black cow from the 'Hall of Bulls' in the Lascaux caves, France

summoned Cuchulainn's spirit back from the Otherworld. Also, the idea of recording the epic on the skin of a cow recalls the method of incubatory sleep during which, according to one Scottish and several Irish sources, bards used to lock themselves in a dark quiet place, wrap themselves in a bull's hide, in order to receive messages from the Otherworld. (John Matthews, *Taliesin*, pp. 112–13). Among a number of Native American tribes, and among the Scottish bards, it was the custom to enter a shamanic state while reclining on a floor in the dark, either covered by or wrapped in a bull hide.

In several ancient mythologies, the Cosmic Cow, Mother of All, created the universe. The Milky Way and all the starry firmament were said to flow in a rich, endless stream from the udders of this divine cow, who was crowned with the horned moon and daily gave birth to the life-giving sun. Among the beasts depicted in the caves at Lascaux, France, sometime between 17,000 and 12,000 BCE, were several cows and the five huge animals which led the discoverers to give it the name 'Hall of Bulls'. Cow goddesses were venerated throughout the Fertile Crescent in Ur, Babylon, Sumer, and Elam. The Egyptian Mother Goddess Hathor was a cow. She was goddess of maternity, sensuality, art, joyful singing, music, dancing, and love. The goddesses Mehueret, Shentayet, Neith and Isis were worshipped in cow form. And Nut, goddess of death, appeared as a great cow with stars on her belly.

To the Celts, the cow symbolized the sacredness of motherhood, and the mother's milk sustained the life force itself. Milk from a sacred cow was an early form of communion with divinity. Such milk was believed to heal battle wounds, and a mother's milk was said to have curative powers. In matriarchal religion, the

Pictish stone carving of a sacred bull, seventh–eighth century

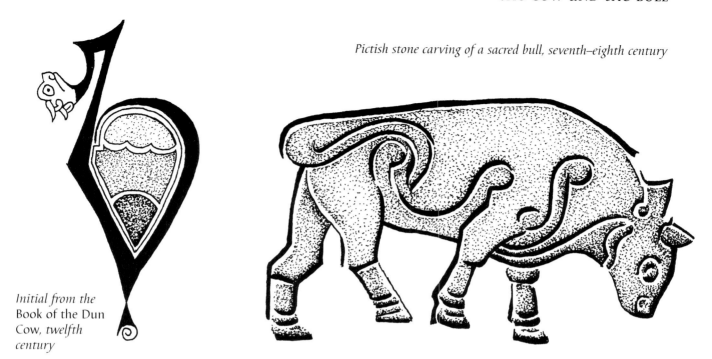

Initial from the Book of the Dun Cow, *twelfth century*

spilling of breast milk was considered as great an offence as patriarchal religion would later attribute to the spilling of semen. Throughout the ancient world, it was believed that breast milk passed on to an infant the spiritual traits of the mother.

The main Celtic divinities associated with the cow were the Irish Boann, the cow goddess after whom the Boyne River is named, and, in her role as Mother Goddess, Brigid, after whom the Brigit, Braint, and

Brent Rivers are named. Throughout the Celtic world, domestic dwellings were usually shared with sheep and cows. Brigid was goddess of both beasts. The name of her festival, Imbolc, referred to the annual lactation of the lambs, and one of her many titles was Bride of the Kine ('cows'), which leads Michael Dames

St Luke from the Lindisfarne Gospels, *seventh–eighth century*

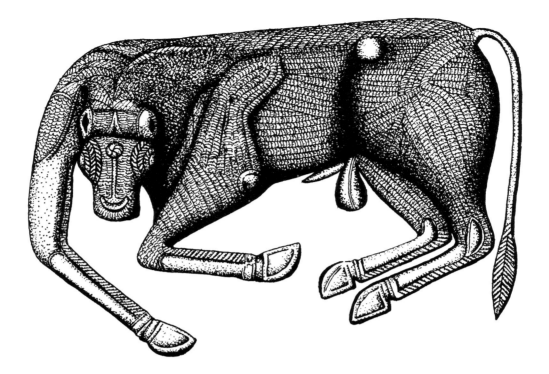

Bull from the Gündestrup cauldron, first century CE

to suggest that she may originally have had the power to *become* a cow. There are numerous legends throughout Ireland about her bovine aspects, and it is possible that the Mound of the Cow at Tara was somehow associated with her Sacred Cow.

An intimate connection with cows is also attributed to St Brigid of Kildare. According to the account of her life in the *Book of Lismore*, her mother was carrying a vessel full of milk when, as she stepped over the threshold of her house at sunrise, she gave birth to Brigid. The attending maids immediately washed the baby with the milk from the vessel still in her mother's hand. After this, a druid provided a Sacred Cow for her lacteal needs, identifiable as an Otherworld creature because of its white body and red ears. This was a clever way of saying that St Brigid bridged the threshold between this world and the Otherworld and between pagan and Christian, while incarnating as a Christian saint a divinity who had both solar and bovine aspects. Cogitosus ua hÁeda records in his seventh-century *Life of St Brigid* that Brigid had cows which could produce a miraculous quantity of milk. Once, when seven bishops arrived unexpectedly, she had nothing to serve them and so she milked her cows

for the third time that day, causing such a flow of milk that it filled a lake, which came to be called the Lake of Milk. She was an expert at dairy work and could both miraculously create large quantities of butter and turn water into milk. On the top of Glastonbury Tor is the tower of what was once the medieval church of St Michael. To this day, a carved panel can be seen on the tower that depicts St Brigid sitting on a stool, milking her cow. This cow remains one of her most enduring symbols.

Cows often appear in the lives of Celtic saints. The fifth-century Irish St Ciaran of Saighir once made seven miraculous cows appear with red bodies and white heads. In the next century, the Irish St Brynach came to Wales and founded several religious houses. At one of them, he kept a cow which gave miraculous quantities of milk and was guarded by a wolf. There once was a conflict between St Cadoc of Llancarfan and King Arthur over protective sanctuary which the abbot had extended to one of Arthur's enemies. When it was settled that Cadoc could ransom the man with a large number of cows, Arthur insisted that they be white cows with red ears. Cadoc complied.

In the Celtic world, bull imagery clusters especially around the deities of poetry, healing, and the Underworld. The bull features strongly in Ireland's creation mythology, and can be seen on coins, in statuettes, and on relief carvings in eastern and central Gaul, Scotland, and England. Carved on a Romano-Celtic altar uncovered in Paris is an image of the god Esus, who is accompanied by a bull with three cranes on its back. This god is connected with a lost myth which concerns the cutting down of trees and the totem animals of the bull and the three cranes. In this context, the cranes and the bull both likely symbolize the Underworld. A fine bronze statue of a three-horned bull has been discovered in northern Gaul. There is a beautiful Pictish carving of a bull at Burghead, Morayshire, Scotland.

At Doohat, County Fermanagh, Ireland, is the 'Ox-tomb' or the so-called 'Tomb of Bith'. Bith, (Irish for 'cosmos, world, eternity, everlasting being, and existence') together with his children Cesair (said to be the founding goddess of Ireland), Anda (or Ladra) and Fintan, was identified as the very first settler of Ireland. He is said to have often reappeared as a bull, prepared to give his life for the communal good.

Until the time of St Patrick, there was an ancient harvest god named Crom Dubh ('the dark, bent one') who was venerated particularly in the provinces of Connaught and Munster, where folklore has it that he owned an immortal bull. St Patrick is said to have once killed the bull by trickery and then to have eaten it. He ordered the bones to be thrown into the hide, whereupon the animal returned to life. Around Galway Bay every household would skin and roast a bull at Samhain in honour of Crom Dubh, and one may assume that Crom Dubh and the bull were originally synonymous (Michael Dames, *Mythic Ireland*, p. 104).

'Ox-cooking' sites are situated in several parts of Ireland and were used well into the Christian era. St Bede the Venerable referred to November as *Blod-monath* ('blood month'), not so much because of the old sacrifices, as because whatever livestock could not be fed throughout the winter was slaughtered and salted down in the first half of that month – often on Martinmas, 11 November. This had a joyous aspect, because it was the last time people would be able to eat unsalted meat until the spring. It also seems to have had some connection with sacrifice. In Ireland, until recent times, one of these animals was offered to St Martin of Tours himself; and it was thought that ill luck would follow the non-observance of this custom. Associated with this was a legend that St Martin himself was once slain, cut up, and eaten in the form of an ox. Here is a case of a former divine animal anthropomorphized into a divinity, which was then merged into the personality of a Christian saint.

There were four great Celtic festivals. Samhain took place on 1 November, Imbolc (Oimelg, or St Brigid) on 1 February, Beltaine (May Day) on 1 May, and Lughnasadh (Lammas) on 1 August. The principal attested druidic ceremony which took place on Beltaine was the driving of cows and bulls between two fires for purification. Livestock emerging from the cold and dampness of winter tended to be sickly and prone to disease. Since fire was considered a purifier, it was used to cleanse them before they were sent to graze for the summer. According to an Irish dictionary – *Cormac's Glossary*, compiled at the end of the ninth or beginning of the tenth century by Cormac Mac Chileannain, Bishop and King of Munster – the word *Beltaine* is derived from *bel-tene* ('goodly fire'). This refers to the purifying fires, which were burned in honour of the god Bel, (Belinus, or Belenos), whose name means 'the shining one'. Bel was a Celtic version of Apollo – god of the sun shining in its strength. On the ancient sacred hill of Belsen, near Tübingen, Germany, there is a twelfth-century church where, inserted into the wall of its west front beneath the cross, are two images of Bel, surrounded by the heads of a bull, sheep, and pigs. They serve as a reminder that the association between Bel and cattle was presumed throughout the Celtic world.

St Luke from the Book of Durrow, *seventh century*

The horse

I**T WAS NOT** only the custom in Ireland to drive cattle between fires at Beltaine, but young men, often naked, would ride horses into bodies of water at Lughnasadh, the great festival of the solar and supreme culture-deity Lugh. Lughnasadh was primarily a harvest and fertility festival. Since bodies of water represented the womb of the goddess, probably the main point of the horse-plunge was the *exiting* of the water, symbolizing birth and new life. The nakedness was probably a reminder of the way the riders would have first come out of their mothers' wombs. Lakes represented divine birth. The solar goddess Aine, whose birthplace was Loch Gur, herself is said to have birthed a divine mare, which emerged from the same Loch and was given to the hero Finn mac Cool.

A horse sacrifice was an essential component in the rites for the inauguration of an Irish king. Giraldus Cambrensis, not the most objective observer of Irish mores, bore witness to the fact that the custom was still being observed at the end of the twelfth century. In 1185, he wrote:

> There is in the northern and farther part of Ulster, namely in Kenelcunill, a certain people which is accustomed to appoint its king with a rite altogether outlandish and abominable. When the whole people of that land has been gathered together in one place, a white mare is brought forward in the middle of the assembly. He who is to be inaugurated... has bestial intercourse with her before all.... The mare is then killed and immediately, cut up into pieces, and boiled in water. A bath is prepared for the man afterwards in the same water. He sits in the bath surrounded by all his people, and all, he and they, eat the meat of the mare which is brought to them. He quaffs and drinks of the broth in which he is bathed, not in any cup, or using his hand, just dipping his mouth into it round about him. When this unrighteous rite has been carried out, his kingship and dominion have been conferred.

Gerald of Wales, *The History and Topography of Ireland*, III:102

In Ireland, the mare represented the goddess of sovereignty, and the monarch had ritual intercourse and communion with her in order to guarantee a proper succession and prosperity to the country. In addition to sovereignty, the horse was a protectress of warriors. Throughout northern Europe, horse sacrifices were

Horses from the Lascaux caves, France

Bronze plaque dedicated to the Celtic goddess Epona, from Alesia, France, first century BCE

considered an essential part of the funeral rites for a dead warrior. They continued to be performed in tenth-century Norway, despite the efforts of the recently Christianized kings to discontinue them. Traces of such rites persisted in England until the fifteenth century, when it was still the custom to bleed horses for luck on St Stephen's Day, the day after Christmas.

The White Mare was worshipped throughout the Celtic world. Among the Gallic Celts she was called Epona. *Epo* is Gallic for 'horse', which is a derivative of the Indo-European *ekwo*, and which also led to the Latin *equus* and the Greek *hippos*. Epona was the only Celtic goddess known to have been honoured in Rome, where she was often called Epona Augusta or Regina. Images of her, half naked, riding her mare side-saddle, often holding a key to the Underworld, have been found throughout Gaul, the German

Rhineland, in many Roman forts and in Rome itself, since she was popular with the soldiers and was invoked on the emperor's behalf. She is sometimes shown carrying a horn of plenty, and is occasionally accompanied by a dog, symbolizing her Underworld aspect. The title Regina ('queen') connects her with her Welsh equivalent, Rhiannon, whose name comes from Rigatona ('Great Queen'). Jean Markale calls Epona 'the true image of the first mother goddess of the Celts'. She was definitely the Great Mother of the Gallic Celts (Jean Markale, *Women of the Celts*, p. 89).

A figure of Epona was found in a well at the Brookes site in Winchester in 1971. While she may have started out as a water divinity, Epona soon

Detail from an initial from the Gospel of St Gatien, *eighth century*

merged with the White Mare and ended up as the divine protectress of horses and asses. Horses were essential to the Celtic lifestyle, and were admired for their speed, strength, and beauty. They were also thought to represent great fecundity and sexual prowess. To a people that considered animals almost an extension of themselves, the horse symbolized the life-force itself. The Gauls were great horse rearers and Epona was goddess of the craft. She was also a deity of fertility, war, sovereignty, and happiness in the after-life, as well as of language and texts.

A horse was sacrificed by the Celts and the Teutons during the mid-summer festival. While Teutons made their sacrifice to Freyr, the god of fertility, the Celtic sacrifice was in honour of the vegetation-spirit and benefited all domestic animals. The connection between the horse and the fertility of the land is apparent in England, where there are great horses literally carved on to the land's surface. One of the best known British hill-cut figures is the 370-foot (100-metre) long White Horse of Uffington, Berkshire; this was probably connected with worship of Epona. In Ireland, there

was a horse temple on Uisnech Hill, which included a stable for the solar horses. Under its paved floor were two elaborate sets of tunnels, whose forms can be recognized as a colossal mare pursued by a great stallion, similar in shape to the horse at Uffington.

As another facet of the horse's relationship to the sun, the solar chariot was said to have been pulled by divine horses. In medieval Denmark, despite condemnation by the Church, peasants took part in a three-day horse-feast, which included a ritual sprinkling with horses' blood towards south and east – the direction from which the horse, as an incarnation of the spirit of the solar year, appeared daily. There are many surviving examples of ancient British coins, on which an amazing variety of solar disc symbols are depicted with horses in the air, some with wings.

The goddess Brigid had a solar, as well as a lunar, aspect. According to *Cormac's Glossary*, one of Brigid's many titles was Breo-saigit meaning 'fiery arrow'. This reference identifies her with the first ray of sunshine, which appears on the horizon at Winter Solstice. In Ireland, when this ray is viewed from the Uisnech Hill, considered the umbilicus of Ireland, it passes directly over Croghan Hill, near where St Brigid is said to have been born and received her episcopal ordination from St Mel, Bishop of Ardagh. Beyond Croghan, the ray passes first through Brigid's main shrine at Kildare, with its famous adjoining Curragh (Currac means 'race-course', or 'plain'). The Curragh pastures have always belonged to Brigid and are famous to this day for horse racing. In ancient times, those races were a sacred obligation, whose purpose was ritually to urge the Winter Solstice chariot across the sky.

The lives of the Irish saints sometimes describe Brigid in a chariot coming from Heaven to Kildare, and her pre-Christian equine form perhaps lived on as the *lair bhan* ('White Mare'), until recently paraded at Midwinter in the form of a hobby horse (Michael Dames, *Mythic Ireland*, p. 229).

The Welsh horse goddess Rhiannon is often depicted as a White Mare rising from the sea with the sunrise. She crests with the breaking waves and can be seen in their foam. Since the sea is the realm of the god Manannán (after whom the Isle of Man is named) and he is also god of the Underworld, Rhiannon too is a powerful Otherworld figure. She is, in fact, the Queen of the Otherworld and Lady of the Night, who appears

The Morrigan

Shapeshifter

Journey to the Otherworld

Epona

Guardian of the Forest

Life Spirit

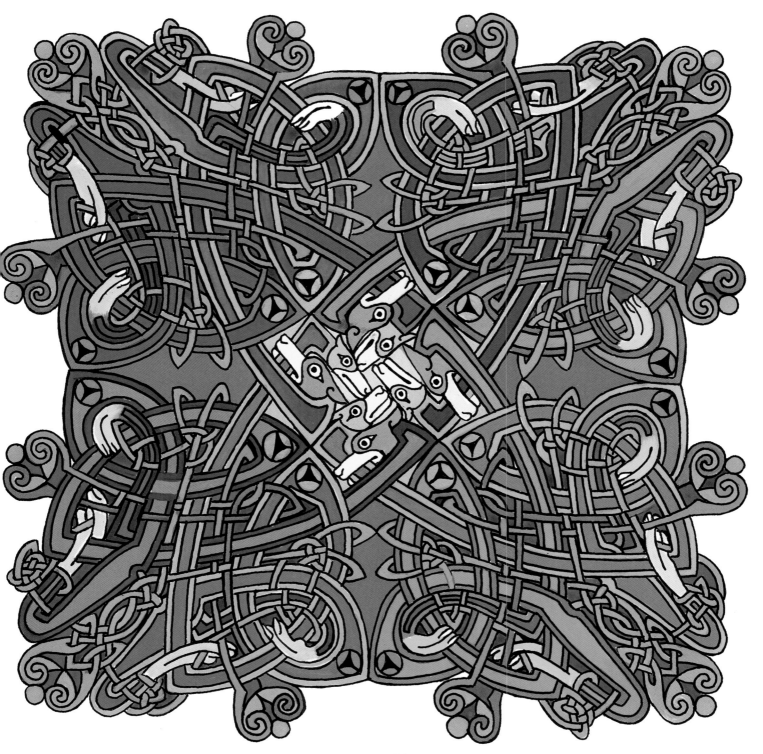

Entwined dogs

The deer's cry

as the Queen of Elfland in the story of Thomas the Rhymer. In her darker aspect, the White Mare is the Night Mare, who haunts dreams, raising Underworld shadows to frighten sleepers into waking up terrified. She is also a muse, who can entrance people when they hear the siren sounds of her seven bird companions. These birds are described variously as small birds, such as tits, warblers, and finches, and as white swans or doves; they sometimes appear as blackbirds or ravens. Hearing the song of these creatures, some people forget their sorrows, others experience a healing of their pains, and others are even said to be raised from the dead. Rhiannon is also the British love goddess, who, like her Greek counterpart, Aphrodite, is born on the waves.

Epona's Irish equivalent is the goddess Macha. According to legend, Macha was compelled by the King of Ulster to race against the fastest horses in Ireland while she was pregnant. Her death at the winning-post, while giving birth to twins, is the reason for the name of the great mound of Emain Macha ('Twins of Macha') in County Armagh. The name commemorates not only the legend, but probably also an ancient ritual. The tale may be a representation of the Neolithic mother goddess being delivered

Billion coin of the Coriosolites, from northwest France, first century BCE

in bondage to the warlike Celtic newcomers. Emain Macha, a site which dates back to before 3,000 BCE, was the political capital of pre-Christian Ulster, abandoned in the fourth or fifth century. Adopted as a Celtic goddess, Macha continued in her maternal aspect but also became the destructive Winter Hag, under whose auspices Ulster became the supreme province of winter and battle. Ard Macha ('Macha's Height') was considered to be Macha's ancient fortress. St Patrick chose it as the site for his principal church, which, under its more familiar name of Armagh, became the seat of both the Catholic and Protestant primates of Ireland.

Horses had a significant role in the lives of several Celtic saints. St Columba had a beloved white horse who intuited that the abbot was about to die and nuzzled him in farewell while weeping on his shoulder. His disciple, St Aidan of Lindisfarne, was once given a horse by his dear friend, King Oswine. Aidan loved both the horse and the gesture, but he gave it to the first beggar he met, later explaining to the disappointed Oswine, 'Surely this son of a mare is not dearer to you than that Son of God?' The Welsh St Collen obtained some land through riding its boundaries on a horse sent by God.

The Uffington White Horse, Berkshire, a first-century representation of the Celtic goddess Epona

The salmon and the eel

THE SALMON, WHICH probably appears more often than any other creature in the Celtic bestiary, is always associated with wisdom and the acquiring of knowledge. In several Irish tales, the home of the ancient salmon is a mythical pool named Connla's Well of Segais, which can be found

Eagle feeding a salmon, from the Cross of Drosten, Forfarshire, Scotland

under the sea in Fairyland, or the Land of Eternal Youth. At the pool's edge grow the Nine Hazels of Wisdom. According to myth, their blossoms, foliage, and fruit would all burst forth at the same hour and drop into the pool. The water would turn into a royal surge of purple. The salmon's wisdom would increase every time they ate the hazelnuts that had fallen into the water. (This also explained the purple colour of the salmon's belly.) In the Underworld six streams of wisdom spring forth and return to Connla's Well; a seventh is said to have become the Shannon River, the longest river in Ireland.

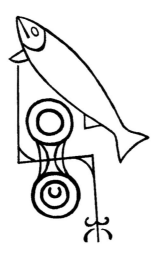

Incised symbols on a pillar stone at Edderton, Ross, Scotland

In the Gaelic version of the Hebrew myth of the Tree of the Knowledge of Good and Evil, only the divine salmon, known in Celtic tales as the Salmon of Knowledge, had the privilege of swimming in Connla's Well and eating the purple hazelnuts. Prompted by curiosity, Boann dared to disobey this fixed law. As she approached the well, the waters rose up against her, driving her off in a rushing flood. She escaped with her life, but the waters never returned. They became the Boyne River, where the salmon wander disconsolately through the river's depths, seeking their lost hazelnuts in vain.

During a later period, when the ancient holy wells and springs were renamed after various Christian personages, the salmon would often reappear as a type of smaller fish, usually trout, but sometimes eels. There are two adjoining wells in Walshetown, County Cork, called Mary's Well and Sunday's Well. The former contains a trout and the latter an eel. Both are considered sources of wisdom and healing. While the holy wells have never lost their association with wisdom, they have also become connected with healing, which is said to take place whenever a pilgrim sees a salmon, trout, or eel appear in the water. There is an ancient connection between wisdom and healing. Both were considered the special gifts of Brigid, who was also goddess of wells and springs.

The salmon also appears in Pictish symbolism. It can be seen on a stone from Easterton of Riseisle, Morayshire, carved in the late sixth century CE. At St Vigeans, Angus, a salmon is depicted beneath a fish-eagle, as though the eagle is feeding the salmon. This symbolic combination of powerful Upperworld and Lowerworld beasts signifies either the height of intellect nurturing the depths of wisdom, or the two directions

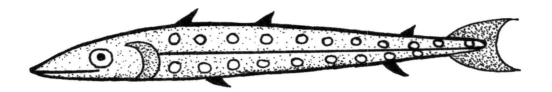

in which shamans make their Otherworld journeys.

The importance of the hazelnut in Neolithic ritual deposits proves the antiquity of its supernatural associations. A connection between the hazelnut and wisdom was presumed as late as the end of the fourteenth century, when the great mystic Julian of Norwich had a revelation in which she experienced all of created reality as 'something small, no bigger than a hazelnut, lying in the palm of my hand' (Julian of Norwich, *Showings*, Paulist Press, New York, 1978) sustained only by the love of God.

The salmon was easily adopted as a symbol important to Celtic Christians. Because the Greek word *ichtus* ('fish') was used as an anagram for the Greek creedal statement 'Jesus Christ, Son of God, Saviour' as far back as the second century, the fish had been accepted as a

Above: The fish as a Christian symbol on a tombstone at Fuert, Roscommon, Ireland

Right: Latin-type cross with a human head and fish tail, from Riskbuie, Argyll, Scotland

symbol for Christ. Also, like a holy well, the baptismal pool was considered a source of life. New Christians were sometimes even called *pisciculi* ('little fish') and the baptismal pool the *piscina* ('fishpond'). Also, when Jesus multiplied the loaves and fish, they were considered anticipatory Eucharistic symbols, and so the fish also came to be connected with the Eucharist.

Walter and Mary Brenneman point out that:

> There is one more important factor peculiar to the salmon, the eel, and Jesus that is decisive in providing the possibility for a syncretism between Celt and Christian. Let us begin with a symbolic examination of the salmon. What is distinctive about the salmon in relationship to other fish is that it lives in the sea but leaves the sea and enters a freshwater river to mate. In other words, the salmon is a boundary crosser, which by crossing the boundary is able to bring about transformation and new life. Further, the boundary crossed is from salt to fresh water, symbolically from the feminine to the masculine, from earth to sky. It is important to note that the river to which the salmon returns is the place of its birth.

Initial from Vallicelliana Ms B62, eighth century

The eel is also a crosser of boundaries. It, too, moves from salt to fresh water and back again, but the process is in the reverse order to the salmon. Thus, the eel spends most of its time in fresh water, then at night crawls on its belly across the land to the sea off the Bermuda Islands where it breeds. The origin of the eel is in the sea, the salmon in the rivers. The salmon, in accordance with its place of origin is masculine, the eel feminine, and together they form the totality of the gods. Both eel and salmon are mercurial figures, bringers of transformation, wisdom, and life.

Walter and Mary Brenneman, *Crossing the Circle at the Holy Wells of Ireland*, p. 78

Individually and together, because of their symbolic gender shifting and the fact they are both boundary-crossers, salmon and eel are symbols of androgyny and completeness. They represent the union between heaven and earth which took place in Christ's Incarnation. They also serve as a reminder that the Celts were non-dualistic in their thinking. They are useful Christian symbols in that they embody the divine Christ's crossing of the boundary between life and death, destroying death's power through the Resurrection. The Celts honoured the eel not only as a purveyor of wisdom and inspiration but also as a protector. The Morrigan herself, goddess of battle and procreation, assumed the shape of an eel during a magical combat with Cuchulainn.

In the past, holy wells in Wales at Ffynnon Gybi, LLangybi, (Caernarfon), Ffynnon Gybi at Holyhead (Anglesey), and in the churchyard at Llandeloy (Pembroke) were said to house sacred eels which could predict recovery by coiling around of the legs of patients standing in their water. The well at Llangybi was considered an important healing centre at least back to the time of St Cybi in the mid-sixth century. Eels were also used for divination. In the past, movements of an eel in Ffynnon Elaet (Anglesey) were interpreted by someone skilled in the art, and people waited for it to appear in order to know what was predicted.

THE DEER

FROM THE FREQUENT appearances of deer in Celtic mythology and in the lives of the saints, it is apparent that these creatures played an important role in Celtic culture. The deer's grace, beauty, swiftness, and keen scent was deeply appealing to a people who continued to rely on hunting as well as agriculture for survival. The Celts believed that such a creature could easily lead one into and out of the Otherworld.

The deer was one of the forms preferred by the shapeshifting Celtic fairies, the Tuatha de Danaan, when they appeared to people, especially in the form of a White Doe or White Stag. They served as Otherworldly messengers for hunters who might come upon them and then find themselves led deeper into the woods and on to great adventures. In the tale of Pwyll, Prince of Dyfed, Pwyll's encounter with a White Stag leads to a meeting and exchange with Arawn, the Welsh God of Annwn, the Underworld. One of the hero Fionn's Otherworldly wives, Sadbh, was said to have been turned into a fawn by a druid, but may originally have been Sadbh, the Irish deer goddess. After fleeing her home, she gave birth in the wild to a son, whom she named Oisin ('little fawn'). Afterwards, his father, whose real name was Demne ('small deer'), found this beast-child in the woods and, recognizing him as his own son, took care of him until his animal nature was less apparent. Oisin

The White Stag

grew up to become a great hero and bard, and his mother retained the ability to shapeshift into a deer whenever she crossed over to the Otherworld. Oisin's son was named Osgar ('he who loves the deer'). They all came from Leinster, part of which is called Osraige ('people of the deer'). The White Hart that Galahad encountered and the golden-collared White Stag Lancelot encountered both betokened Christ.

In continental Europe, St Eustace and St Hubert were both said to have been converted to Christianity while hunting, because of visions they had of stags with crucifixes between their antlers. The hind, which St Giles once protected from hunters, is portrayed in art as his companion to this day.

Several Welsh saints had domesticated stags. St Cadoc's principal monastery was called Llancarfan, which means 'Church of the Stags'. It acquired its name when two of Cadoc's monks lazily refused to help construct the monastery, complaining to him that they were not oxen to be yoked to a cart and compelled to draw timber. Just then, two stags came out of the woods and performed the service the monks refused to do. St Iltyd likewise tamed a stag, which he employed to pull a wagon full of timber for his own church building. St Teilo used stags to pull a cart. St Ieuan Gwas

Stag from the Lullingstone hanging bowl

Padrig was led by a roebuck to the site of his monastery. St Oudoceus protected a stag from hunters.

Saints Brynach and Taithi, both Irish monks living in Wales, had tame stags. One of the earliest followers of the Irish St Ciaran of Clonmacnois was a doe. He also had a stag companion, which allowed him to use its antlers as a book stand. A stag likewise pulled the chariot of the pre-Patrician St Declan of Ardmore. St Patrick himself, along with seven others, once shapeshifted into deer.

Among the Celts and the Anglo-Saxons, there was unquestionably a stag cult, which lasted well into the Christian era. In one of his epistles, St Aldhelm (d. 709 CE) mentioned the stags, which in earlier days had been worshipped in pagan shrines. He abhorred the customary wearing of animal costumes (especially stags), a tradition which was continued by contemporary revellers. Reminders of this once pan-Celtic cult have lasted in many locations until recent times, and are continued to this day in an arcane Christian blessing and in a well-known dance, the Staffordshire Abbots Bromley Horn Dance.

There were very few cults more important to the Celts than that of the horned god, who was an anthropomorphized stag. In imagining this divinity, as in so many other aspects of their sacred symbolism, the Celts drew from the beliefs and symbols current in northern Europe and elsewhere in the prehistoric Bronze Age. The horned god was primarily Lord of the Forest and its creatures, a bringer of fertility, rebirth, healing, and Lord of the Underworld. There are several reasons for believing that he was equivalent to Dis Pater ('Father Dis'), to whom, according to Julius Caesar, all Gauls traced their ancestry. Dis Pater was a god of wealth, fecundity, and the Underworld, possibly a patriarchal displacement of the ancient grain goddesses.

The Celtic Underworld was envisioned as place of fertility and light. The new grain, which was seen regularly to sprout from the ground, brought nourishment and prosperity. One of the reasons deer were associated with the Underworld was that they were grain-eaters. Since in the cycle of life, people are born

Stag caught in a trap, from an eighth-century stone slab at Banagher, Ireland

Gallo-Roman relief of Cernunnos, second century BCE

from a womb and buried in the earth, the Underworld was thought to be not only the abode of the dead but the great womb of rebirth, inspiration, and creativity. Anne Ross points out that the horned god may have been a syncretism of several of 'the gods of a hunting or pastoral, warlike people, their leader in war, symbolic of fecundity and virility, lawgiver in times of peace, protector in times of danger, an all-purpose tribal god.' (Anne Ross, *Pagan Celtic Britain*, p. 214.)

There are many depictions of horned gods which date back to prehistoric times. The earliest Celtic example comes from the fourth century BCE and is located at Val Camonica in northern Italy. This simple image includes the symbols which are most typically associated with this god in Romano-Celtic sources: the horns, serpents and torc. The horned serpent is often his companion and appears thus at Val Camonica. While the

god himself is not phallic in this depiction, his worshipper is markedly so. The horned god was worshipped all over Gaul when the Romans arrived. They themselves made images of him, in which he sometimes holds a bag or purse (interchangeable with a cornucopia), which is also a symbol of Mercury. This purse further identifies the horned god with the Roman god of the Underworld, for his name, Pluto, is from the Greek *Plouton* which means 'wealth' or 'riches'. There is one known relief inscription, the only one thus far discovered, which actually mentions the horned god's name. The stone with this inscription was found in Paris and identifies him as Cernunnos, but the name and image of Cernunnos are preserved in several British sources and legends in which he appears either as Cerne the Hunter, or Herne the Hunter, the antlered woodland creature who is said to live in Windsor Forest.

The equivalence of Dis Pater with the Roman Pluto, and the similarity of both to Cernunnos, is all background to a syncretism which might help to explain the fuller meaning of a unique and curious Christian blessing still given annually in many churches, the blessing of throats on St Blaise's Day. St Blaise absorbed the gods Volos, Pluto, Hades, and Cernunnos. Dis Pater can be added to this list, and, just as Dis Pater had probably displaced some of the older grain protectresses, so, in parts of medieval France, St Blaise was the only male saint to stand in their place when it was time to bless the fields. Both in France and in Belgium, he was associated not only with the fertility of the fields but also the fecundity of women. (Pamela Berger, *The Goddess Obscured*, pp. 81–4.) Cernunnos represents the fertility of the mind as well as the body. In many cases where he has been depicted naked, the horned god is without a phallus. It has been pointed out that one of the things a serpent can signify is the rush of energy, which uncoils from the root of the spine and ascends to the top of the head, leading to an explosion of pure enlightenment. Since it is an interior orgasm, the phallus is interior. Just as in Kundalini Yoga, energy can uncoil up the spine and bring an interior explosion of insight, so the spine is the channel through which human imagination connects with the genital area and can lead to stimulation and external orgasm. The throat is the channel through which both these energies pass, the place where the horned god wears his torc and where St Blaise's blessing is given for healing and protection. St Blaise's Day follows immediately after the fire feasts of St Brigid and Candlemas (recall that Brigid was goddess of healing, therapy, and the bards). The horned god was associated with healing, and the throat is the channel through which the bards declaimed their truth. The actual blessing is given in a peculiar way. The one giving the blessing takes two candles blessed on Candlemas and holds them at the recipient's throat, so that they form a cross similar to St Andrew's, but with the upper parts longer than the lower. Simultaneously a blessing is said in the saint's name. There is no clear evidence that the blessing was given in exactly this way from before the time of St Francis de Sales (d. 1622), who encouraged its use as part of his effort to eradicate some of the even more manifestly pagan customs along the Swiss, Italian and French borders, but it is possible that, if these two candles could trace their genealogy back far enough, they would eventually shapeshift back into the stag horns on the head of Cernunnos. This might appear a rather startling conclusion, until we note that devotion to the originally beneficent horned god had such an enduring hold on Christians that his 'Christianization' by the Church proceeded in two directions: he either shapeshifted into St Blaise or into the medieval horned devil. Thus was the stag demonized along with the serpent.

On the famous Gündestrup cauldron in Copenhagen's National Museum, a figure which some have identified as the horned god appears seated, with branching antlers, surrounded by animals over which he was particularly powerful, among them a stag, a boar, and a wolf. In his left hand, he holds a ram-headed serpent and in his right a torc. He also wears a torc on his throat. A strikingly similar figure is carved on the north column at Clonmacnois. Some have questioned, however, whether this is really Cernunnos and might not actually be a shaman, wearing the antlers and holding the paraphernalia of his calling. Such shamanic tools were used in Celtic Britain. Deer horns, once from a shaman's ritualistic headgear, have been found with part of the skull intact in Star Carr, England. They date back to between 8,000 and 7,500 BCE.

The wolf and the hound

EVEN THOUGH THE wolf was extinct in all parts of England by the end of the fifteenth century, in Scotland a century later, and in Ireland by the eighteenth century, its place in Celtic lore and art was already secure. It appears as a companion of the horned god not only on the Gündestrup cauldron, but also on a carved slab from Meigle, Perthshire. Two wolves can be seen on the Market Cross at Kells, standing on both sides of an upright, naked, bearded, bull-horned man, who grasps their tails.

Because of their nocturnal wanderings in forests with eyes that shine in the dark, and because they feed on corpse-flesh, wolves were considered useful guides to and from the Underworld. Since they were good hunters, able to survive in the wilds, they were thought to be particularly helpful spirit guides for shamanic journeys. They would have been able to help

a shaman survive in the Otherworld and to track down whatever needed to be discovered or recovered. Because wolves howled at the moon, they were considered sacred to the moon goddess. Robert Graves claims that, in addition to being the great sow goddess of the Underworld, the Welsh Cerridwen was a wolf goddess as well. (Robert Graves, *The White Goddess*, p. 222.) According to J.A. MacCulloch:

> There were various types of underworld gods, and this wolf-type – perhaps a local wolf totem ancestor assimilated into a local 'Dispater' – may have been the god of a clan who imposed its mythic wolf origin on other clans. Some Celtic bronzes show a wolf swallowing a man who offers no resistance, perhaps because he is dead. The wolf is much bigger than the man, and hence may be a god.
>
> J.A. MacCulloch, *The Religion of the Ancient Celts*, p. 218

Detail from the eighth-century Hilton of Cadboll Pictish slab

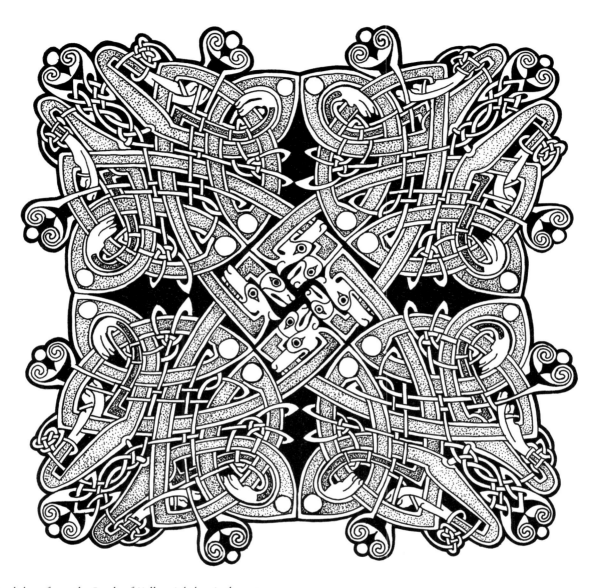

Entwined dogs from the Book of Kells, *eighth–ninth century*

This might reflect a belief that people return to their totem ancestors after death and are thus, symbolically, devoured either by the ancestor or by the Underworld divinity connected with the ancestor. Thus the totem animal of Dis Pater, from whom all Celts claimed descent, was Blez, the wolf. It would follow that everyone of Celtic ancestry might also be part wolf. No wonder the idea of the werewolf is so compelling.

It may be that, before they were demonized, werewolves were originally considered helpful and necessary ambassadors of peace between humans and the wolves. Robert Graves pointed out that:

The Arcadian religious theory is that a man is sent as an envoy to the wolves. He becomes a werewolf for eight years, and persuades the wolf-packs to leave man's flocks and children alone during that time.

Robert Graves, *The White Goddess*, p. 359

The extensive research of folklorist Arnold van Gennep has revealed that in many places throughout France and Belgium, a wide variety of local sayings focus on either the wolf or the bear as the beast whose emergence on Candlemas is used to predict when the winter will actually end. Also associated with Candlemas are many of the Black Madonnas of Europe. These are numerous – over 300 in France alone – and include some of the most famous pilgrimage Madonnas in the world. They have Caucasian features and dark complexions and are usually located where ancient earth goddesses were formerly venerated. The home of the Black Madonna of Chartres is the crypt underneath the Cathedral, located on the site of the most important druidic centre in Gaul. To this day she is called *Notre Dame de Sous-Terre* ('Our Lady of the Underworld'). Another famous Black Madonna is at the cathedral at LePuy, a major druidic centre. On the cathedral's *porche de for* a grinning face can be seen between two wolves.

In 1185, when Giraldus Cambrensis recounted the story about the human couples, who had to do seven-year terms of service as werewolves, one couple after another, he attributed the phenomenon to a curse which St Natalis put on Ossory. The thirteenth-century Norse *Kongs Skuggsjo* ('Royal Mirror') tells the same tale, but in this version the cursing saint was Patrick. When, at the request of the citizens of Gubbio, St Francis of Assisi (1181–1226) acted as an ambassador to a local menacing wolf and tamed it, no one called him a werewolf or treated him with the suspicion that would lead later generations to execute hundreds of thousands of people as witches, sometimes simply because they had a 'way' with animals. Instead, because of his way with animals and his affection for Brother Sun and Sister Moon, Francis has been revered by most of humankind ever since and held up as a supreme model of ecological connectedness.

Among the Celts, the hound was known primarily as a hunting animal. On Pictish carvings, dogs are most frequently depicted as part of the hunt. Because of their scenting and tracking skills, combined with a near-human instinct, dogs were considered as ideal companions for people in this life and spirit guides in the Otherworld. Hounds are depicted in various other aspects on the Gündestrup cauldron, and on the base panel from the North Cross at Ahenny, County Tipperary. The Crozier of the Abbots of Clonmacnois (*c.*1100), a masterpiece of Irish metalwork found in the tomb of St Ciaran, has five beautifully formed hounds climbing the curve of its top. Dogs are among the favourite beasts with which monks graced the pages of illuminated manuscripts. Fine examples can be seen in the *Book of Kells*, and the *Lindisfarne Gospels*.

Perhaps because it howled at the moon, the dog was sacred to the lunar goddess. The Greek goddess of the dark moon, Hecate Triformis, was imaged as a triple goddess and represented as a three-headed dog. This is a reminder that, at an earlier time, she herself was originally the Moon-dog. She carries a torch, symbolic of the moonlight, through which she gives the special gift of fertility. One of the reasons for the triple aspect in her Greco-Roman manifestation is that she had power in all three worlds of the shamanic universe. Like any other watchdog, the Greco-Roman three-headed hound Cerberus was considered to be the guardian at the entrance to the Underworld. Finn mac Cool had as his companions two hounds of semi-human origin. The Ulster hero Cuchulainn gained his name 'Hound of Culainn' after overcoming and then taking the place of a huge hound. After many heroic exploits, Cuchulainn finally died after being tricked into eating dog flesh, thus violating his *geas*, a taboo which forbade him to ever eat the flesh of his own power animal

By the Middle Ages, the kind of imagination which had led to the belief that people who could communicate with wolves were werewolves, also nurtured a belief in the existence of monstrous races of various other sorts. Encyclopedists had a great time describing them. Embellishers like the Irish enjoyed nothing better than to hoodwink gullible, biased writers like Giraldus Cambrensis by regaling them with such legends. Of course Giraldus then recorded them as facts. Probably the best known of these hybrid humans were the Cynocepha Li, or the Dog Heads. Pliny wrote that they lived in the mountains of India. They could not talk and communicated by barking; they wore animal skins, lived in caves, and hunted efficiently with normal human-style weapons. They may simply have been cave-dwelling indigenous inhabitants, who had never before been seen by Europeans. St Albert the Great (d. 1280) related them to the great apes in his own writings, which hints that they may indeed have been Aborigines. Many Christian writers wrote about them and numbered them among the nations for whose sake the Saviour died and rose. An Armenian gospel illuminated in 1262 shows a Dog Head among the figures to whom Christ is preaching, as does the eleventh-century *Theodore Psalter* now in the British Museum (Adam Douglas, *The Beast Within*, p. 106).

The pig

For at least the 8,000 years since the beginning of the Neolithic Age, the sacred animal of Mother Earth has been the pig. Pigs were probably seen to be related to the earth because they are rapidly growing, fattening, and highly prolific animals. Their growth and fecundity were compared to the abundance of the harvest. (Marija Gimbutas, *The Civilization of the Goddess*, p. 229.) In some places, ancient pig figurines have been found with signs of impressed grain; and some vegetation goddesses have been found wearing pig masks. A continuous relationship between pigs and the grain spirit is revealed in folklore. It is not an accident that the English word 'sow' is both a noun for a female pig and a verb which means 'to scatter seed over land'. To this day the Rajput Clan of northern India worships the Corn Mother Gauri ('abundance') in the form of a pig (Buffie Johnson, *Lady of the Beasts*, p. 262).

In Crete, the Crone, as goddess of wisdom, took the form of a sow. The Celtic Hag, the Cailleach of Winter, likewise was often thought of as a sow. In ancient Egypt, the god Set, as a boar, killed his brother Osiris. The sky goddess Nut, who swallowed the stars at dawn in order to birth them at dusk, was known as 'the sow who eats her piglets'. An Upperworld goddess described as a sow is unusual. More often, precisely because it liked to wallow in mud and was capable of devouring its own offspring, the sow was considered a major Underworld beast.

In ancient Greece, the primary ploughing and sowing festival, the Thesmophoria, was dedicated to Demeter and took place in October. Like Brigid's festival of Imbolc, it was celebrated exclusively by women. At

Detail of a boar carved in sandstone, first century BCE

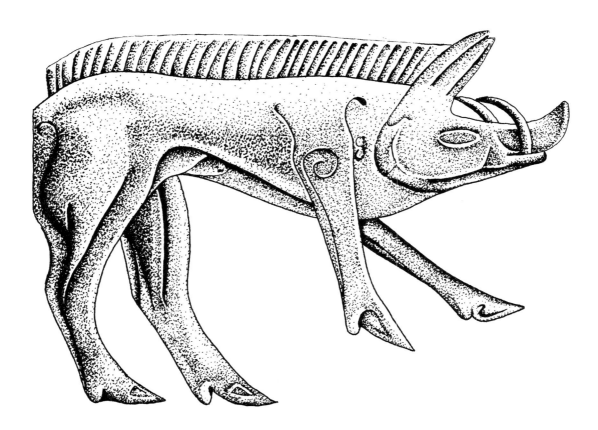

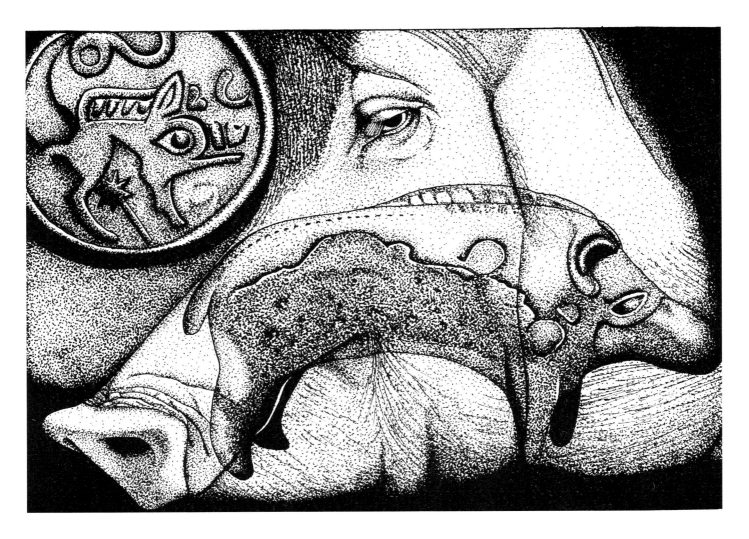

Coin from the Somme basin, France, first century BCE. Bronze helmet crest in the form of a wild boar, from north-east Wales

some time before the feast, as a preparation, piglets were hurled into chasms in the earth, in honour of Demeter and her daughter Kore ('The Maiden', or Persephone). Also thrown in were pine cones and cakes baked in the shape of male genitals. The high moment of the Thesmophoria came when specially selected women descended into the chasms and carried up the rotten piglet remains, which had not yet entirely been devoured by the snakes in the chasm, and laid them on the altar of Demeter and Kore. The snakes were representatives of the Earth Mother and, as guardians of her inner sanctuaries, generally viewed as privy to the mysteries of the Underworld. Those who could obtain part of the rotten piglet flesh and mix it with their seed were guaranteed a good crop. The Thesmophoria rites were also meant to aid animal and human fertility. (Pamela Berger, *The Goddess Obscured*, p. 17.)

A British version of Demeter/Ceres was found in the Welsh goddess Ceridwen. Anne Ross claims that she came to Britain with the New Stone Age agriculturists

from North Africa between 2,500 and 2000 BCE. (Anne Ross, *Pagan Celtic Britain*, p. 222.) Called the Great White Sow, into whose Underworld cauldron all souls had to return for inspiration and regeneration, she was a shapeshifter, the Underworld initiator, and goddess of inspiration. The great sixth-century bard Taliesin seems to have encoded the steps of his shamanic initiation in his poetry. There he specifies that the mysteries into which he was initiated were those of Ceridwen. The phases of this process were symbolized in the transformations through which he passed, from when he was named Gwion Bach until he was reborn of Ceridwen and named Taliesin

Though the pig was not one of the goddess Brigid's totem animals, her namesake St Brigid did have a pet boar. Many of the tales surrounding Brigid involve miraculous multiplication, similar to Jesus' multiplication of loaves and fishes. She is once said to have miraculously produced a large quantity of pork. As the Irish goddess of wisdom, Brigid was the revered keeper of the sacred cauldron of inspiration, healing, therapy, and rejuvenation. If there was any place in Ireland where Brigid's cauldron could be located, it was Croghan Hill. *Croccan* means, 'vessel, pot, or cauldron', and Brigid, who was also goddess of metallurgy, was said to form her Underworld pots, and the cauldron from which both the future and the River Shannon were poured, beneath Croghan Hill. This is where her namesake St Brigid would be born and eventually ordained. Brigid was also goddess of the hearth and its fire. It was the custom in many parts of Ireland to bury a cauldron under the hearthstone, thus making it possible for each home to have its own symbol of the abyss, the lower hemisphere, which was her world. Such miniature 'Underworlds' have been found under floors in counties Clare, Kerry, Limerick, and Tipperary.

The pig was the beast sacred to the ancient Celtic Mother Goddess, Anu (Danu), worshipped in Ireland before the Milesians arrived. When the sons of Mil came in their ships and were about to invade, the Tuatha de Danaan (people of the goddess Danu) are said to have caused a magic fog to rise, which gave the island the appearance of an enormous pig. Hence it came to be called Inis na Mulce ('Isle of Pig') or Muc Inis ('Hog Island'), before it received its present name.

Because pigs came from the Underworld, they were considered sure guides for shamanic journeys. Pork was the favourite meat of the Celts and was considered the principal food of the Celtic Otherworld and of Norse Valhalla (the hall where heroes slain in battle feasted and revelled for eternity). Druids were particularly fond of pigs because they liked to eat acorns, the produce of the sacred oak. A pig was one of the animal familiars of the second 'Merlin', Myrddin Lailoken, who was a druidic seer living in a primarily Christian world. In ancient Ireland, in order to obtain needed information, a seer would sometimes chew on a piece of the flesh of a pig which had been sacrificed to the proper god. Then he would wrap himself in the hide, hoping to obtain some of the deity's knowledge through entering into a trance.

According to Anne Ross, 'the boar is, without doubt, the cult animal *par excellence* of the Celts'. (Anne Ross, *Pagan Celtic Britain*, p. 390.) It was even more important than the bull in Irish mythology. One piece of evidence that the boar was sacred to the Celts prior to the Roman conquest of Gaul is in the claims of the writer Pytheas, that Orkney (Old Norse for 'pig islands') was already known as *Orcades* (from *orci*, meaning 'young pigs') by the fourth century BCE.

The boar was the national symbol of the Gauls and appeared on their standards and their coins. The Franks used it as well, until it was displaced by the *fleur-de-lis*. The name of a god Moccus ('Pig') was discovered at Langres and seems to have been equated with Mercury. Among the Vikings, boars and horses were sacred to Frey, god of fertility, and boar's flesh was eaten for sexual potency. Warriors on the Gündestrup cauldron wear boar crests on their helmets, and gods depicted in one of its panels hold boars aloft. A boar was the most frequently used animal on the terminal of a carynx, a Celtic trumpet, connecting boars with warfare, which is appropriate to their ferocity.

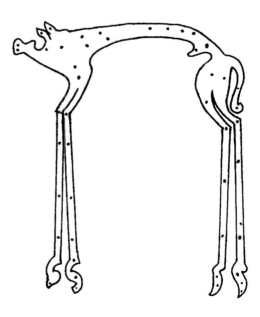

Boar from the Witham shield, first–second century CE

Other mammals
The Cat

Cats appear only occasionally in Celtic myths, an exception being the tale 'The Voyage of Maelduin'. During this adventure, the voyagers encounter a seemingly harmless kitten. When one of the crew tries to steal some of the nearby treasure, the cat turns into a fiery arrow, which strikes him and reduces him to ashes. According to *Cormac's Glossary*, one of Brigid's names was Breo-salgit, meaning 'fiery arrow', and it is possible that it was she who was guarding the treasure in the form of a cat. Her lavish hospitality and the white cloth she wore are characteristic of her. Indeed Maelduin himself was said to have been a Leinster man, whose mother came from St Brigid's Kildare. In this story, the cat was understood to be a good guardian and possibly a protector of inner powers as well.

There was a cat cult in Ireland before the arrival of St Patrick. At Clough, in Connaught, there was an oracular cave shrine, whose prophetess was 'a Slender Black Cat reclining upon a chair of old silver'. This cat gave vicious answers to anyone who tried to deceive her. (Robert Graves, *The White Goddess*, p. 221) There was a similar shrine in a Knowth burial chamber, County Meath, whose resident, the King Cat Irusan, was said to have been as big as an ox. Irusan is said to have once carried the chief bard Senchan Torpest away on its back in revenge for a satire, the bardic tool for heaping scorn on any patron who crossed them.

Because they are depicted on some Gallo-Roman funerary monuments in an Underworld setting, cats also seem to have had a chthonic aspect. Scottish Highlanders believed in the Cath Sith, or 'the Cat of the Sidhe' (the Otherworld abode of the fairies). This cat was believed to be a shapeshifted sorceress, full of esoteric knowledge. In Ireland, the flesh of a cat (or a dog, or red pig) could be chewed as part of a method of divination. Unfortunately, during the European Middle Ages, cats were persecuted. They came to be associated with witches and divination and inquisitor Nicholas Remy declared all cats demons. Efforts were made in parts of France and other places in Europe to exterminate not only the hundreds of thousands of women accused of sorcery, but the entire cat population. Shrove Tuesday, Easter, and Midsummer were favourite times to burn cats in wicker cages.

Possibly the primary reason cats can be found on the pages of many illuminated manuscripts is that they made fine house pets and useful pest controllers in the places where monastic scribes lived and worked. The ancient Egyptians also loved their domestic cats, and they venerated the cat goddess Bast as the manifestation of the sun's gentler life-giving and life-enhancing aspect. She is a particularly beloved, quintessential mother figure.

Cats with mice holding the host from the Book of Kells, *eighth–ninth century*

The Lion

Even though there is little evidence that larger cats had much place in the Celtic world, the fact that the symbol of Mark the Evangelist was a lion and that Daniel in the lions' den was a subject suitable for illustration, gave the monks all the outlet they needed to guarantee lions a permanent place in any Celtic biblical bestiary.

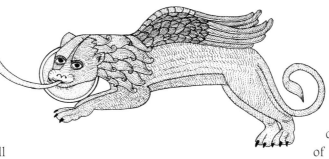

Symbol of St Mark from the Lindisfarne Gospels, *seventh–eighth century*

Lions are associated with many deities throughout the world. The ancient Mother Goddess Cybele was originally depicted as lion-headed and then later envisioned as a female with attending lions. The Egyptian Sekmet remained a lion-headed goddess, ruling over the fierce noonday sun and the Tablets of Destiny. She was goddess of fertility and a protector of the young and the weak, and also a divinity of war and destruction. The goddesses Ishtar and Astarte also rode or drove lions. There are lions depicted on the Gündestrup cauldron. Even though lions are not native to Britain, the legendary lost lands off the Cornwall coast are called 'Lyonesse' after one of its queens, appearing in Arthurian romance as Lady Lyonors. In several ways, this drowned land is reminiscent of Atlantis. The Welsh city of Caerleon means, 'The Lion's Place'. Depictions of Cybele, enthroned between two lions, arrived in Britain on Roman coins. Her mural crown eventually became the Saxon emblem of divinity. To this day, a lion is one of the two totem animals supporting the coat of arms of Great Britain.

Detail from twelfth-century arch at Tuam, Galway, Ireland

The Hare

Julius Caesar wrote that hares (and geese and cocks) were held in awe by the British. It is important to know this, because there is little other actual evidence of the hare's significance to the Celts. Just before she began her campaign against the Romans, Queen Boudicca of the Iceni released a hare from beneath her garment, while invoking the Iceni goddess of war and victory, Andraste ('Invincible'), and divined the outcome of the battle by the hare's manner of flight. Otherwise in Britain, hares were sacred to the moon goddess, and Boudicca's banners depicted the beast in this capacity. Hares were also dedicated to the Saxon goddess Eostre (Easter) at her spring rites, hence the modern tradition of the Easter bunny. An ornament in the Cashel cathedral, County Tipperary, Ireland, shows a couple of hares complacently feeding on tri-lobed foliage such as shamrock. However, the unfortunate hare usually appears as quarry in many carvings of hunting scenes.

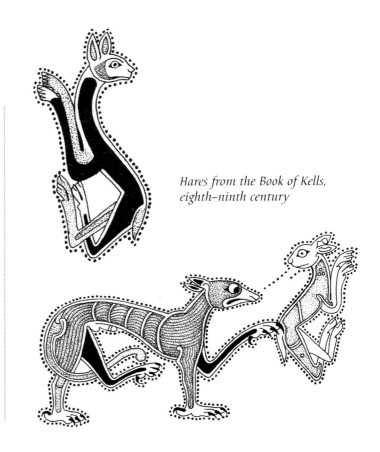

Hares from the Book of Kells, eighth–ninth century

The Sheep

By the Middle Ages, the wool industry was important in several parts of Ireland and Britain. The goddess Brigid and her saintly namesake were both fond of sheep and served as their protectoresses. The name of their main festival, Imbolc, refers to the lactation of the lambs. Dedications to Brigid's saintly associate, Blaise, began to appear in places where there was a thriving wool industry, because he was its patron saint. In addition to Kildare, whose nuns were famous for their weaving, there was an area around Boxgrove Priory, near Chichester, which was dedicated to St Blaise and St Mary, as was St Blazey in Cornwall. In medieval art, the symbol used most frequently to identify Blaise among other bishops was his wool comb, with which he was supposedly tortured during his passion.

The Ram

The association of the ram with Celtic war gods is well attested. The Belgic war god Camulos was worshipped at Colchester (the old Roman name was *Camuloddunum* meaning 'Fort Camlus') and depicted as ram-horned. A fine example of this kind of head was found at Netherby, north of Carlisle. The ram is depicted with warriors' deities found at Lower Slaughter, Southbroom, and Stow-on-the-Wold in Gloucestershire. The ram-headed serpent has a chthonic aspect and is often a symbol of the horned god.

Birds

The Eagle

Sculpted on one of the stones at St Vigeans in Angus is a design depicting an eagle feeding a salmon. According to Nicholas Mann, the combination represents the heights of intellect nurtured by the depths of wisdom. (Nicholas Mann, *The Keltic Power Symbols*, p. 34.)

Together, they also represent the shamanic universe and the two directions in which it is possible to go when journeying. Eagles and many other birds can serve as ideal spirit guides to and through the shamanic Upperworld.

The eagle has been regarded as the greatest of birds by many people. Its size, power, beauty, and apparent ability to fly right into the sun made it both a supreme Upperworld guide and an obvious symbol of solar divinity. The

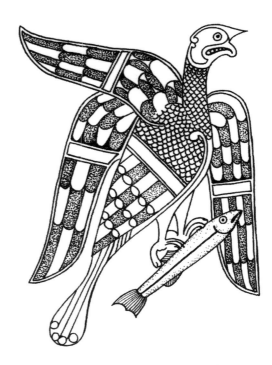

Eagle of St John from the Book of Armagh, *eighth–ninth century*

Eagle on a seventh-century incised slab at Birsay, Orkney

Greek Zeus, his Roman counterpart Jupiter, and the entire Roman Empire were symbolized by eagles. They appear frequently on Celtic cult objects and coins. The eagle is the totem animal of Taranis, (the 'Thunderer'), Jupiter's Gallic equivalent. An eagle scratched on a bone plaque at Lydney Park, Gloucestershire, indicates that it was associated with thermal waters. In both Irish and Welsh traditions, the eagle is listed as one of the oldest animals. The Irish eagle of Druim Brecc and the Welsh eagle of Gwernabwy belong to this tradition. The latter was consulted by Culhwch and his companions in their search for Mabon ap Modron (Maponus). Part of the eagle's response is:

> I have heard nothing of the man you seek. Except that one day I went to Lynn Llyw to seek my food. And when I came there, I sank my talons into a salmon, thinking he would provide me with food for a long time ...
>
> Ann Ross, *Pagan Celtic Britain*, p. 350

The Pictish stone at St Vigeans may have been intended to illustrate this scene. The legendary Irish seer, Fintan, spent one of his lives as an eagle. So did Tuan mac Carell. The Hawk of Achill is said to have engaged in a debate with an eagle over which of them remembered the coldest winter. After he was killed, the spirit of the Welsh divine solar hero Lleu, the equivalent of Lugh, flew off in the shape of an eagle. Maeldrin and his companions witnessed an eagle renewing itself in a secret lake. Among the Norse, an eagle representing the shamanic Upperworld was perched on top of the sacred tree of Yggdrasil.

The Raven

Anne Ross describes the role of the raven in Celtic tradition as follows:

> The role of the raven in the entire Celtic tradition at all stages, as a bird of omen, possessing outstanding intelligence, and as a creature particularly concerned with the battlefield is such as to cause it to be associated with any deity accredited with exceptional knowledge, skill and martial abilities.
>
> Anne Ross, *Pagan Celtic Britain*, p. 320

The Morrigan ('Phantom Queen') was the terrifying Irish triple-goddess of battle, procreation, death, sexuality, and conflict. Her other two forms were Nemhain ('Frenzy') and Badhbd ('Crow' or 'Raven'). In the 'Tochmarc Emire' (an episode from a group of tales known as the 'Cuchulainn Cycle') she is described as the battle crow. Likewise the name of the fierce Macha can mean 'crow'. The raven-goddess of Gaul is Nanto-suelta. In Gaul, Epona too may have raven-goddess associations. In the thirteenth-century Welsh tale 'The Dream of Rhonabwy', there is an entire army of immortal ravens. Cuchulainn was unsuccessfully wooed by the Morrigan in her raven aspect. The Germanic Odin is always accompanied by the two ravens of wisdom and knowledge. It has been suggested that, because of his name, the Celtic titan Bran ('Raven') originated as a raven-god; but there is no real proof of this. His story appears in the tale of 'Branwyn, Daughter of Llyr'. When he is mortally wounded, he requests his men to behead him and bury his head on the site of the present Tower of London as a palladium which will guarantee the nation's security. Around this story developed the legend that if the ravens ever leave the Tower, Britain will be invaded.

Sixth-century helmet plate from Vendel, Sweden, showing a rider, possibly Odin, with an eagle-crested helmet, accompanied by an eagle and a raven

The Hawk

In the Middle Ages, the hawk (whether a kestrel, falcon, kite, or eagle) was flown for sport. While most of Celtic tradition presumes that the salmon is the oldest and wisest beast of all, one tradition makes the same claim for the Hawk of Achill. The hawk as a symbol of transformation was one of the forms into which Gwion Bach shifted on his way to becoming Taliesin. Fintan also passed one of his lives as a falcon. At Woodeaton in Oxfordshire, there was a Romano-British temple of unknown dedication. Here, as at Lydney Park, Gloucestershire, archeologists have found many representations of birds, all apparently either hawks or eagles. They seem to have been connected with a healing cult. St Cadoc considered a hawk at the top of a tree part of a sign that he had arrived at a correct site for one of his foundations. St Taithi persuaded a kite to return a pet pigeon which it

The Hawk

had stolen from him. Gawain's British name was Gwalchmai, or 'Hawk of May'. And a merlin, the name used both for Merlin Ambrosius and Myrrdin Lailoken in literature, is a type of falcon. Giraldus Cambrensis reported that a tame falcon lived at Kildare, perching on a church tower, from the time of St Brigid, but that the beloved creature, called 'Brigid's Bird', was killed by an ignorant local around the year 1183.

The Crane

The crane is no longer native to Britain, but it is deeply rooted in Celtic tradition. It was considered a magical Otherworld creature, because of its secrecy, patience, and trance-like way of resting. One of the wonders of Ireland was said to have been a crane which had lived on the island of Inis-Kea, County Mayo, from the beginning of time and would remain there until the Last Judgement. Cranes which appear in most Celtic tales show an aggressive streak. The legendary Fairyland King Midir is said to have possessed three sinister cranes, which kept all visitors to his dwelling at bay by warning them to go away. They were generally regarded as the guardians of the gates to the Otherworld. On a relief found at Risingham, Northumberland, Victory is shown standing on a globe, beneath which is a crane. In Gallo-Roman carvings, cranes are sometimes associated with Mercury and sometimes with Mars. They appear on cheek-pieces and shields, probably for protection, and are connected with a Gallic vegetation deity named Esus, also called Silvanus. The infant Finn mac Cool was said to have once been rescued by his divine grandmother in the form of a crane. Otherwise the crane is almost exclusively associated with transformed, aggressive women. This seems to have led to a superstitious dislike for it long after its cultic significance was forgotten. The Irish and Scottish Highlanders had an aversion for crane flesh, and in this part of the world unpleasant old women were apt to be called cranes. Thus did the symbolism descend from crane-as-goddess to crane-as-witch.

St Columba had great respect for cranes. He once correctly predicted that a crane was about to be stranded on Iona and sent a monk to the shore to rescue it when it arrived. However, when a queen scornfully referred to him as a 'crane cleric', he turned her and her maid into herons. It has already been noted how Columba was touchy about his druidic training. He was proud of it, but he didn't think that it perfectly complemented his Christianity, so he felt

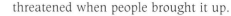

The crane

threatened when people brought it up.

In his book *Taliesin*, John Matthews carefully looks at every recognizable hint of what went on at the various phases of bardic initiation and makes the following observations about the crane's relationship to the process:

> It is possible ... to attempt a tentative reconstruction of the original initiation ceremony, as it might have been performed long since, in both Britain and Ireland. After imbibing a drink which contained some drops of blood from a sacrificial bull, the would-be aspirant had to leap over a cliff (perhaps blindfolded) to show his faith in the goddess he served. She, in her crane form, caught him, preventing him from falling to the ground and being severely hurt. If he was already in a drugged state, as a result of drinking the potion, and if the cliff were not too high, he could easily have jumped down without too much hurt and with all the sensations of flying. He was then vouchsafed a vision of some kind, probably involving the dancing of the Crane Dance.... In this he may have danced with the Goddess herself and at the end was presented with the crane-bag as a symbol of his initiation, the contents of which represented the aspect of the poet's or shaman's art.
>
> John Matthews, *Taliesin*, p. 86

The first crane bag was made by the ancient Irish sea god Manannan mac Lir as a receptacle for the ancient Hallows of Ireland. It was formed of the skin of his son's mistress, Aoife, who had been turned into a crane because of her jealous behaviour. The bag was passed on from Manannan to Lugh, thence to Cool, and finally to his son Finn. Later 'crane bags' seem to have been like medicine pouches, which contained whatever implements a bard needed to make shamanic journeys, enabling him safely to bypass the cranes guarding the entrance to the Otherworld. Symbolically, the crane bag was the repository of the entire Celtic bardic tradition.

The Goose

Because of their belligerence, geese were usually associated with war divinities. They are depicted with the Gallic Mars in his sanctuary at Roquepertuse, France. A goose appears below a representation of Mars on a slab from Risingham, Northumberland, and they can be seen in Scotland on the walls of caves in Fife. A goose is depicted above a salmon in a late sixth-century carving on a slab from Easterton, Scotland. Another appears with a mirror (a goddess symbol) on a slab from Tillytarmont, Aberdeen, and yet another flies into the eye of a warrior on a stone from Aberlamno, Wales. A fourth-century funerary tile from Roussas, France, shows a hag-like Epona riding on the back of a horned goose, hinting that she is probably the ancient ancestor of Mother Goose.

Garrett Island, in Ireland's Lough Gur, is now a wild-fowl sanctuary. In folklore, it is the Otherworld home of Gearóid (Garrett) Iarla Fitzgerald. As a goose, his spirit still haunts the lough. And to this day, he is called 'Goose of the Island'.

Gearóid Iarla was both a fourteenth-century Earl of Desmond and a bard, who wrote fine Irish verse. His poems seem to indicate that his wife's excesses made him a great cuckold; but he took it in his stride. His historical wife actually seems to have been virtuous; so he may have been referring metaphorically to Ireland. His father had made several unsuccessful bids for the High-Kingship. Gearóid Iarla may have seen himself as some sort of latter-day Hosea, like the Hebrew prophet, comparing his wife's faithlessness to his nation's. But in this case, the faithlessness was to himself, rather than to God.

Another indication of his desired connection with sovereignty is noted by Máire Cruise O'Brien. Recalling the ancient inauguration custom of a monarch's ritually mating with a white mare as a consummation of his relationship with the goddess of sovereignty, she points out that after the custom died, the bards symbolically carried on the role of the goddess. 'In bardic poetry this practice is refined to a convention of romantic attachment between the ruler and the poet, in which the poet plays the role of the woman.' (Máire Cruise O'Brien, 'The Role of the Poet in Gaelic Society' in *The Celtic Continuum*, p.250.) The sixteenth-century bard Eochaidh O'hEoghusa did this. Similarly, the earlier Gearóid Iarla dedicated his verses to his great freind and probable foster-brother, Dermot MacCarthy, in the role of a bard addressing his lord:

> Gearóid's goosiness was applied to the Fitzgerald family as a whole; they were said to have webbed feet, and a song from Co. Waterford refers to 'Gentle Aine Fitzgerald', close relative of a swan.
>
> Michael Dames, *Mythic Ireland*, p. 111

The Swan

There are several Irish tales of divinities transformed into swans, who are recognizable because of their golden chains. A swan maiden appears in the eighth-century tale 'The Dream of Angus'. Cuchulainn is also involved with several maidens in swan transformations. In the tale, the 'Wooing of Étain', Midir and Étain both become swans. The four children of Lir are also turned into swans by the druidic skill of their jealous stepmother. After 300 years, they meet the missionary St Mochaomhog, who introduces them to Christianity. They join him and become his mass choir. When the Queen of Connaught demands the birds from him and he refuses, the king snatches them from the altar. They immediately turn into ancient people, whom the saint baptizes, after which they die. Swans always have beneficient associations in the Celtic world. Their skin and feathers were used to make the bard's ceremonial cloak of office, thus aligning his poetic function with the musical language of the birds. Because St Hugh of Lincoln (d. 1200) had a beloved pet swan, they are kept on the cathedral grounds to this day in his memory. The Benedictine monastery of St Peter in Abbotsbury, Dorset, was famous for its swannery. The abbey is long gone, but the swans continue to thrive at what is now the largest swannery in England.

Birds from the Book of Kells, *eighth–ninth century*

Celtic and christian syncretism

S T Patrick was a Romano-British Celt. Even though his father was a deacon and his grandfather a priest, he seems to have taken both his Christianity and pre-Christian religious roots for granted until his kidnapping and enslavement in Ireland. During those years of solitude, he learned to pray, simultaneously deepening his Christian faith and his appreciation of the religious sensibilities and the spirituality of Celtic paganism. He became more aware of the ways in which the two faiths were compatible.

While the ancient Celts had numerous deities, they generally did not try to depict them in images. They considered divinity to be so much greater than humanity that such depictions would more impede than assist a person in relating to any deity. It was primarily under Roman influence that images of anthropomorphized Celtic deities began to appear, and attempts were made by people like Julius Caesar to find exact parallels between Celtic and Roman goddesses and gods. This was a difficult task, because the Celtic divinities were so broad and overlapping in scope that the boundaries delineating and identifying them were more vague than their Roman counterparts. The Celts tended to experience balance and completeness when things

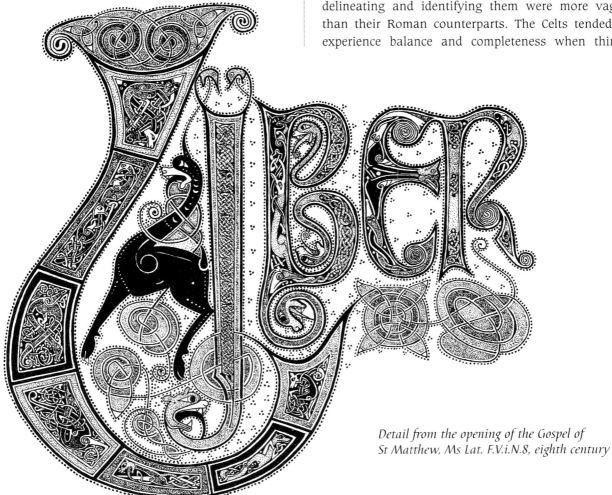

Detail from the opening of the Gospel of St Matthew, Ms Lat. F.V.i.N.8, eighth century

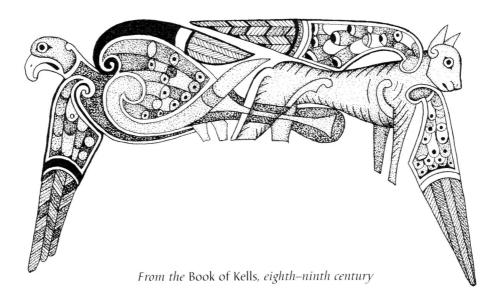

From the Book of Kells, *eighth–ninth century*

were numbered or categorized in threes, so they sometimes thought of their goddesses as having a triple aspect, thus also emphasizing the incomprehensibility of deity to limited human understanding. Some examples are the triple-goddess Brigid, the Irish sovereignty goddess Banbha/Fodla/Eriu, and the Irish war goddess Morrigan/Nemhain/Badhbh.

To people who already thought this way, acceptance of the Christian Holy Trinity was not much of a stretch. The Celts not only believed in the Otherworld but also thought that beings from both sides of the veil separating the worlds had an interest in each other's affairs and could pass from side to side in certain circumstances. The idea of Christ's Incarnation and the Communion of Saints were not difficult for them. Knowing these things, St Patrick took a step unique among Christian missionaries and avoided attacking the old deities. Wherever he could, he 'Christianized' them and the places sacred to them. Since the Celts considered divinity too great to be contained in buildings, they worshipped outdoors. Patrick usually did this as well.

The Celtic church leaders who came after Patrick generally followed his example. Many were either druids or trained by druids. St Columba (also Columcille, d. 597 CE) is an example of this. He was a great-great-grandson of Niall of the Nine

From a gold plaque of St John the Evangelist, eighth–ninth century

Hostages, therefore a prince of the royal family which ruled Ulster and whose descendants became the O'Neill's and the O'Donnell's. Under the guidance of one of his teachers, an old Leinster Christian bard named Gemman, Columba became a bard himself. He had a fine voice and composed beautiful verses. In one of his verses he refers to Christ as his druid, and a study of Columba's life will reveal that he used many skills which were considered a normal part of druidic curriculum.

One episode in Columba's life, which occurred while he was establishing his headquarters at Iona, has kept scholars speculating ever since it was first recorded. Before he and his companions arrived there, Iona was a druidic centre, whose ancient name was Inis Druineach, or the 'Island of Druids'. Somehow related to the foundation of the Iona community was the death of St Oran. What scholars can't sort out is the question of how he actually died. The entry about him in *The Book of Saints* reads as follows:

An Irish abbot of Meath who crossed over to Scotland with St. Columba, and was the first to die at Iona. His feast (October 27) is kept throughout Ireland. He is the principal patron of Waterford.

Benedictine Monks of St Augustine's Abbey, Ramsgate, *The Book of Saints*, p. 426

However, Oran is not mentioned among those who accompanied Columba from Ireland to Iona, and all are supposedly listed in the seventh-century *Life of St Columba* by St Adomnán. Some versions say that he was Columba's cousin and that he came to Iona thirteen years before Columba, setting up an earlier Christian community there. According to some accounts, when Columba arrived at Iona, he was greeted by men who claimed to be Christian bishops but who, on closer scrutiny, were pagan druids. Oran was possibly one of these. In his *Tour of Scotland*, published in 1774, Thomas Pennant recorded one of several versions of an old story in which Oran sanctified the ground by allowing himself to be ritually killed and buried. After three days, Columba had desired a farewell look at his friend and caused the earth to be removed:

> To the surprise of all beholders, Oran started up, and began to reveal the secrets of his prison-house; and particularly declared, that all that had been said of hell was a mere joke. This dangerous impiety so shocked Columcille that with great policy he instantly ordered the earth to be flung in again, poor Oran was overwhelmed, and an end forever put to his prating.
>
> James Charles Roy *Islands of Storm*, pp. 156–7

John Matthews refers to the same incident, observing that, long before its Christian foundation, Iona was recognized as an Otherworldly island. He points out that the Oran story is a clear enough indication of the

Eagle of St John from the Lindisfarne Gospels, *seventh–eighth century*

way pagan shamanic beliefs were beginning to be treated under the influence of people like Columba, who were not comfortable with areas where druidic teaching appeared to contradict Christian doctrine. Nevertheless a study of the lives and deeds of the Celtic saints clearly reveals a considerable degree of shamanic activity. (John Matthews, *The Celtic Shaman*)

It is not invalid to conclude from the Oran story that it might be an example of the way shamanic journeying continued to be practised by Christians like Columba and his companions. In such a case, it was not a

From the Book of Kells, *eighth–ninth century*

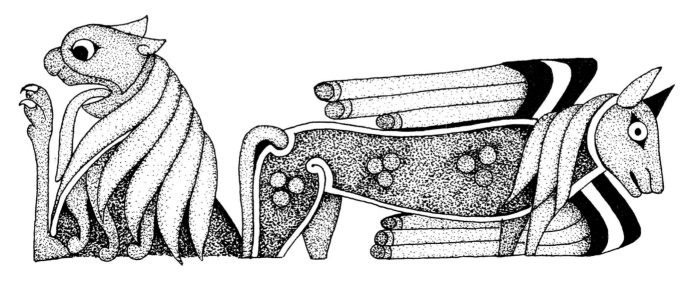

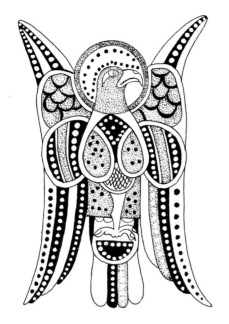

From the Book of Dimma, *eighth century*

From the Lichfield Gospels, *eighth century*

question of literal death, but of a person being assisted by another in making a spirit journey to the Otherworld for the purpose of obtaining useful knowledge, otherwise unavailable through more ordinary means. Usually this was done by companions who trusted each other. The one going on the journey might need help in finding his way back to this world, perhaps through the drumming of his companion. Otherwise, if he got lost on the other side, he might remain there.

There is a parallel between what Oran revealed about the Otherworld and what contemporary people who have had 'near-death experiences' relate about what they recall from brief periods during which they have been clinically dead. Their accounts are usually supportive of the belief that there is indeed life beyond bodily death and, at the same time, challenging to the more frightening traditional descriptions of death and judgement offered by some denominations.

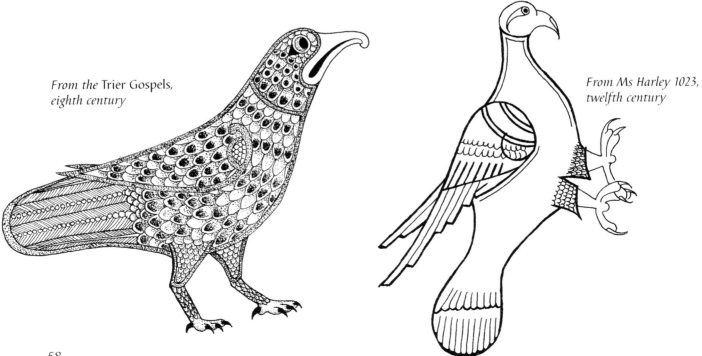

From the Trier Gospels, *eighth century*

From Ms Harley 1023, twelfth century

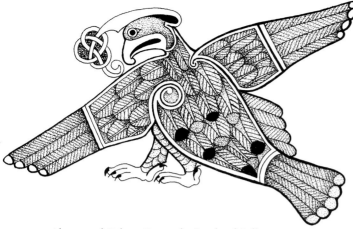

Above and Below: From the Book of Kells, *eighth–ninth century*

However one regards the St Oran story, Columba doesn't come off very well in it. When Oran begins to reveal that the Otherworld is more like the paradise known to ancient Celts than the harrowing experience with which some Christian preachers were beginning to frighten believers, Columba finds the revelation altogether too challenging to his adopted Christian understanding of afterlife, so he quickly dispatches the messenger back to the Otherworld.

In addition to shamanic journeying, another trance-like state into which people might enter was the incubatory sleep. In many ancient places, when physicians had no other means of figuring out either a diagnosis or a proper treatment, they would sleep in the temple of a deity associated with healing, hoping that an answer would come to them in dreams. This was done in the temples of Asclepius at Epidaurus and of Rome. After Christianity's arrival in Rome, the custom shifted to the church of the physician saints, Cosmos

and Damian. In the Celtic world, Christians continued to use pagan temples for this purpose. There were incubatory sleeping chambers in the temples of Nodens at Lydney Park, in Gloucestershire.

At the end of the fifth century, a Christian couple named Amon and Anna made a long journey from South Wales. Their destination seems to have been Scotland's Loch Maben temple, whose prophet they consulted concerning their inability to have a child. This resulted in the miraculous birth of St Samson (d. 565 CE), whose own teacher, St Iltyd, would be called in the sixth-century Life of St Samson 'by descent a very wise Druid' and whose son became a famous missionary to Brittany and first bishop of Dol.

From the Book of Kells, *eighth–ninth century*

From Corpus Ms 197b, seventh–eighth century

From the Echternach Gospels, *690 CE*

Having treasured learning from ancient times, Celtic monks and nuns placed a high value on knowledge, had an unquenchable thirst for books, and tried to assemble great libraries in their establishments. Since these monasteries and convents also had scriptoria for the copying of books, the tales, traditions, laws, and history, which had always been passed on in an exclusively oral tradition, began to be written down for the first time ever. For a Celtic writer, trained in the bardic tradition, it was never enough simply to copy words. The bards always embellished their narrations with facial expressions, verbal elaborations, fluctuations in vocal tone, sound effects, and music. The skilful use of these tools had a mesmerizing effect on audiences and drew then more deeply into what was being recounted. Demonstrating the same skills their forebears had used in wonderful, imaginative designs on metalwork and stone carvings, the Christian scribes embellished their texts with glorious colours and elaborate details.

From the Echternach Gospels, *690* CE

From Ms Harley 1023,
twelfth century

Capital letters and edges of pages are often so filled with zoomorphic designs that a person studying the page and captivated by its beauty can be drawn into a place more like the Otherworld than like this world, and more like the afterlife experienced by St Oran than the one anticipated by St Columba. Columba himself had a great reputation as a scribe. Still in existence is his famous *Cathach*, said to have been a personal Psalter, which may have been written in his own hand. If the work is indeed Columba's, then apparently even he couldn't resist the impulse to grace some of the capital letters with animal heads. In the great manuscripts which followed later in history, beasts, foliage, flowers, and people are whimsically interwoven with each other in a mystical way not usually experienced on this plane.

From the Book of Armagh, *eighth–ninth century*

From its beginnings, Christianity was comfortable with the use of religious symbolism, especially as a means of teaching people who could not read. By established tradition, certain beasts came to be associated with Christ, his mother, and the saints. For example, either a fish or a lamb might represent Christ, a dove the Holy Spirit, or a deer drinking from a stream the human soul yearning for God. Celtic scribes had great fun weaving some of these symbols into the designs in their manuscripts.

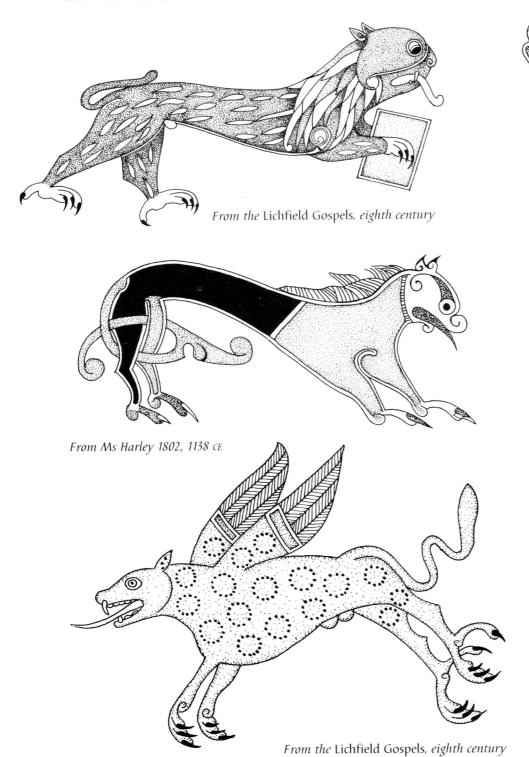

From the Lichfield Gospels, *eighth century*

From the Macdurnan Gospels, *ninth century*

From Ms Harley 1802, 1138 CE

From the Lichfield Gospels, *eighth century*

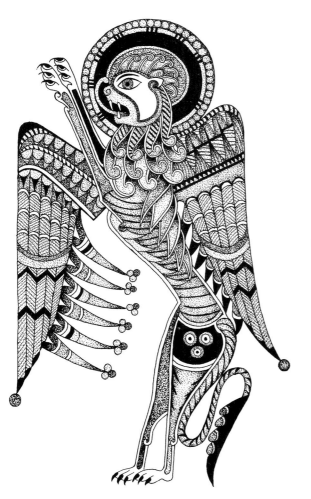

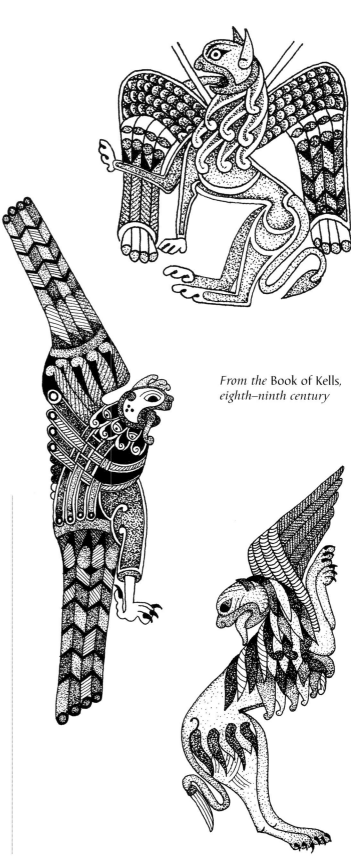

From the Book of Kells, *eighth–ninth century*

By far the most frequently reproduced symbols were those representing the four evangelists: a human for Matthew, a lion for Mark, a bull for Luke, and an eagle for John. These four creatures first appear together in the opening chapter of Ezekiel, a priest more prone to psychedelic visions of a shamanic sort than any other Hebrew prophet. At the core of his inaugural vision of the presence of God, he describes seeing the following:

And round the throne, on each side of the throne, are four living creatures, full of eyes in front and behind: the first living creature like a lion, the second living creature like an ox, the third living creature with the face of a man, and the fourth living creature like a flying eagle. And the four living creatures, each of them with six wings, are full of eyes all round and within, and day and night they never cease to sing, 'Holy, holy, holy, is the Lord God Almighty, who was and is and is to come!

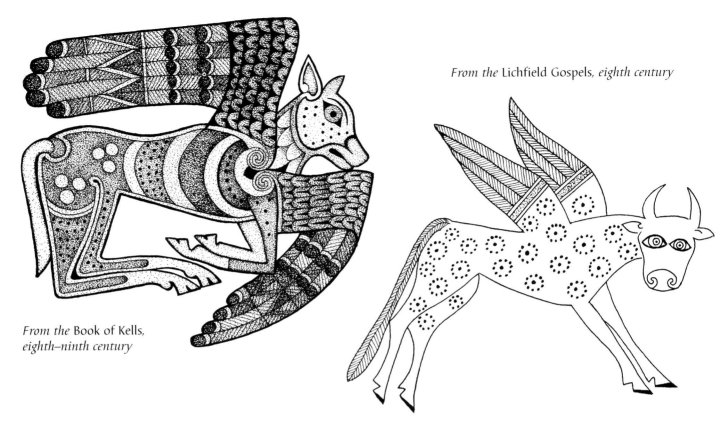

From the Lichfield Gospels, *eighth century*

From the Book of Kells,
eighth–ninth century

Scripture commentators taught that these faces were to be understood as aspects of the indescribable presence of the one God. They believed that God inspired all the scriptures, of which the four gospels constituted the Christian core. So they considered Ezekiel's four faces to be apt symbols for the individual evangelists and the God who inspired them. They used the starting point of each gospel to guide them in making the specific assignments. Because Matthew began with the genealogy of Christ, the human was assigned to him. Since Mark began with a voice crying in the wilderness, the lion was deemed his appropriate symbol. Because bulls were sacrificed in the Jerusalem temple and Luke began with the priest Zachariah ministering there, the bull became Luke's symbol. And because John began his Gospel with a magnificent, soaring, poetic outburst, the eagle was thought to suit him perfectly. This means that, among the beasts favoured by the Celts, the lion, the bull, and the eagle would find particular places of honour in illuminated gospel books, in carved stone, and in metalwork.

From Ms Harley 1802, 1138 CE

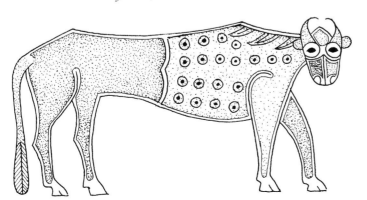

From the Echternach Gospels, *690 CE*

From the Book of Kells, *eighth–ninth century*

65

Hiberno-saxon art

There was very little art produced in the sixth-century monasteries to judge by the little that remains. This is probably a reflection of the simple ideal of the monks at that time, and it was not until the late seventh century, when the monasteries had grown in size and wealth, that there became a demand for religious objects to adorn the altar.

The early sixth- and seventh-century Pictish and Irish artists and craftspeople drew upon a upon a range of styles and techniques from British and European art as a source of inspiration in their book-painting, metalworking and stone-carving skills. The jewellery techniques of filigree, cloisonné, and the new type of ornament, the ribbon, reached northern Scotland and Ireland and were soon adapted onto stone crosses and the illuminated page.

Seventh-century plaque made from antler, with similar style ornament to the Book of Durrow

Because of the restricted material conditions in the Irish monasteries the development of the illuminated books gradually shifted during the seventh and eighth centuries from Ireland to Iona in Scotland, and then Northumbria where they were commissioned by the wealthy Anglo Saxon kings, and from there to Kent. The decorated manuscripts which were produced in Britain and Ireland in the period between 550 and 900 CE are often referred to as 'insular', in recognition of the close interaction of artistic skills between Britain and Ireland. Hiberno-Saxon is used as a term to signify the close links in style by the artists of Northumbria, Scotland and Ireland. On many books which have survived over the centuries it is difficult to tell precisely where they were executed. The *Book of Durrow* is a clear example of

Detail of cloisonné garnets from a shoulder clasp found at the Sutton Hoo burial ship

Two interlaced boars in cloisonné with garnets, from the Sutton Hoo burial ship

Part of a carpet page from the Book of Durrow, seventh century

this: arguments are advanced for a Northumbrian provenance, although there is stronger evidence that it was produced on Iona in the mid-seventh century.

The *Durham Gospel*, an early book from the library of Lindisfarne, is the first to use interlace (which is thought to have originated in Egypt) in its decoration, and a decorative initial letter with double-headed snakes. This manuscript lies between the *Cathach* of St Columba, which is thought to have been produced by the saint's own hand on Iona in the late sixth century, and the *Book of Durrow*. Animal ornament found on the slightly earlier artifacts from the Anglo Saxon Sutton Hoo burial ship are closely matched with the long-snouted, labyrinthine animals to be seen in the *Book of Durrow*, which is the first of the surviving manuscripts to be found completely preserved with its elaborately ornamented pages.

The lion, the symbol of Mark from the Book of Durrow, *seventh century*

Seventh-century Pictish cross slab from Papil, Shetland, showing a dog-like lion with similarities to the lion in the Book of Durrow

From the Durham Gospels, seventh–eighth century

There are many similarities between Pictish sculpture and the Evangelist symbols in the *Book of Durrow* especially with the hip and shoulder spirals on the calf and lion. The artist of this small gospel book shows great skill and assurance with his use of the pen and colour, drawing on several different sources of inspiration which were taken from a common pool of decoration shared by different monastic centres.

The *Echternach Gospels* and *Durham Gospels* were thought to have been produced at the Lindisfarne scriptoria around 690 CE under the direction of the monk Egbert, the possible master of Eadfrith – the scribe to which the later masterpiece of illumination, the *Lindisfarne Gospels*, is attributed. The prancing lion in the *Echternach Gospels* is one of the finest examples of Hiberno-Saxon work, and though similar to the fragment Cotton Ms Otho C.V. in style, the former is superior in artistry.

Though only a fragment of what was once a fairly large gospel book, the richly decorated *Durham Gospels*, dated to the end of the seventh century, was once comparable in the quality of its work to the *Lindisfarne Gospels*.

The *Lindisfarne Gospels* was written by Eadfrith, Bishop of Lindisfarne around 698 CE to commemorate the enshrinement of St Cuthbert, and it is one of the few early gospel books to have survived complete. Along with the *Book of Kells*, they represent the finest achievement of insular art. Alterations in the *Lindisfarne Gospels* are very similar to the hand found in the *Durham Gospels* showing that they may have been at the scriptorium at the same time. The decorative panels reflect the favourite pastime of Anglo-Saxon nobility, portraying realistic hunting dogs, and falcon-like birds of prey with sharp claws. It was associated with the shrine of St Cuthbert and travelled with the saints relics after 875 CE, when the monks were forced to leave their holy island because of Danish invaders.

From the Lindisfarne Gospels,
seventh–eighth century

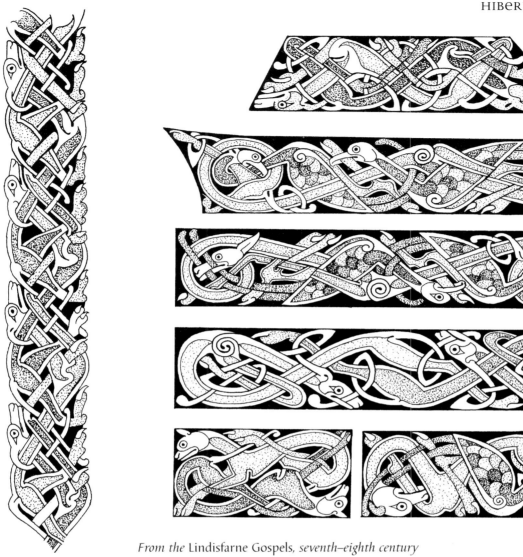

From the Lindisfarne Gospels, *seventh–eighth century*

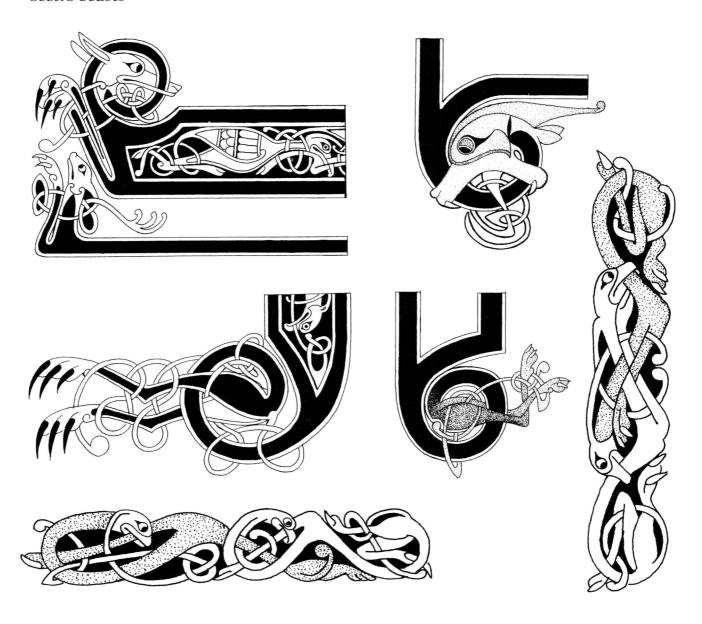

The *Lichfield Gospels* is closely related to the *Lindisfarne Gospels* in influence, especially on the *Christi autem* initial and carpet page. Its script has been described as being between Lindisfarne and Kells. George Henderson, a scribe artist located in Northumbria, suggests:

> ... such is the artist of the *Lichfield Gospels*. I would call him Ultán, if I were pressed for a name. As the 'De Abbalibus' poem says of Ultán, 'He could ornament books with fair marking, and by this art he accordingly made the shape of the letters beautiful one by one.'

George Henderson, *From Durrow to Kells*, p. 26

From the Lichfield Gospels, *eighth century*

The Lichfield manuscript is dated to the early eighth century and is known to have arrived in Wales by the early ninth century. In the early eighth-century collection of canons, Cod. 213, there are no clues to its origin but it was probably produced in Northumbria. It is written and decorated to a standard to impress, and equals the luxury gospel books in its execution. It

From the Lichfield Gospels, *eighth century*

comes from the same tradition as the *Durham Gospels* and the *Echternach Gospels* and was possibly created in the same scriptorium. The manuscript may have been specially commissioned as there is evidence that it was in Cologne by the eighth century. From the ninth century English decorated manuscripts are termed Anglo Saxon.

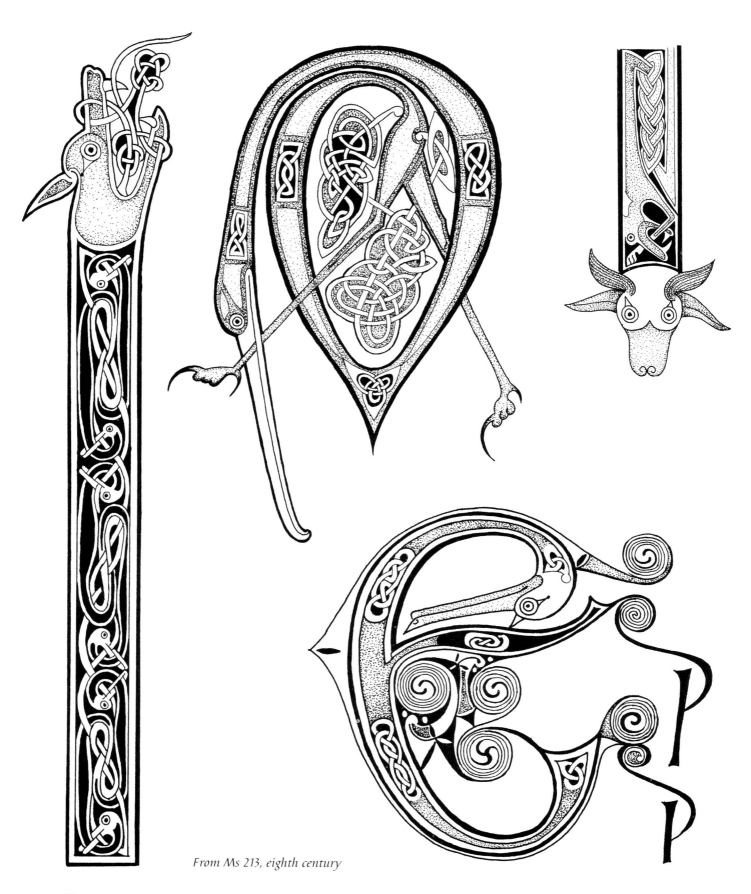

From Ms 213, eighth century

From Ms 213, eighth century

THE INFLUENCE OF VIKING ART ON THE CELTIC SCRIBES

ACCORDING TO IRISH chroniclers, around 830 CE, the Viking Turgesis brought his 'great royal fleet' of fair-haired Norsemen to the north of Ireland and began to found colonies, establishing them at Dubh/Linn at the ford of Liffrey, a stronghold from where they could plunder and burn the great monasteries, and kill the abbots and monks.

Aed Finnliath, the Irish High King, began to fight back and was successful in destroying the Norse strongholds in the north. The Vikings then moved into the middle and south of

Tenth-century Jelling-style silver brooch from Norway

Ireland, ravaging churches and sanctuaries, destroying and stealing precious reliquaries and books as they went. After 880 CE, constant pressure from the Irish resulted in the number of raids diminishing, and there was an uneasy peace in Ireland.

After the battle of Clontarf in 1014, when Brian Boru defeated the Vikings, the power of the Norsemen in Ireland came to an end. A cultural revival in metalwork began, though its quality never matched the earlier work of the Armagh Chalice and Tara Brooch. The new work had many influences, including Scandinavian metalwork techniques and styles, and the beginnings of a true Romanesque art.

Despite the destructive power of the Vikings, and the exodus of many of the Irish scribes to Europe to continue their work, the art of illumination continued in Ireland but in a much weaker form.

The twenty-two gilt bronze bridle mounts found at Oseberg are the earliest remains of a Viking art style and date from the late eighth century CE. As the ninth century progressed, two new styles emerged which were both named after places in Scandinavia. The first was the Borre style, with its ring-chain decoration made up of a double ribbon. This was named after a rich find from a barrow-burial site at Borre in Vestfold, Norway.

The first style to develop from Scandinavian influence was the Jelling style named after a small silver cup found at a Danish burial mound in Jelling, Jutland. It became popular in the late ninth century, and lasted until the late tenth century. Occasionally both the Borre style and Jelling style are found on the same

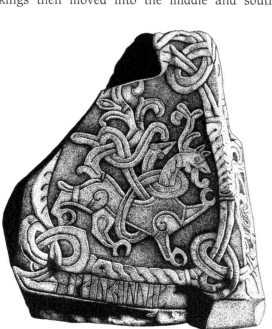

The Jelling Stone. The runic inscription tells that it was erected by King Harald 'Bluetooth' of Denmark in the tenth century

Above: A great beast and serpent on an end-slab of an eleventh-century Scandinavian tomb at St Paul's Cathedral, London

Below: Ringerike-style great beast ornament on a gilt bronze vane from an eleventh-century Viking ship

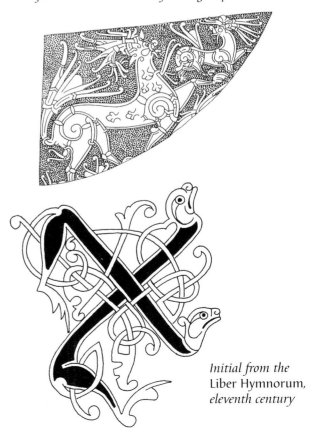

objects. The Jelling style was introduced to Britain by the Scandinavian settlers, who found an art form already based on highly stylized animals which went back to Germanic origins on memorial stones. The new settlers quickly adopted them for their own use, drawing on the Anglo-Saxon traditions and their own style.

In the late tenth and early eleventh century, the Mammen style developed from the Jelling style. This takes its name from a silver inlaid axe found at Mammen in Jutland, Denmark.

The Ringerike style grew from the Mammen ornament, and is more disciplined. In this style the plant design had been expanded upon at the expense of the animals. This style became extremely popular with artists in Britain and Ireland, and one of the finest examples can be seen in the churchyard of St Paul's Cathedral in London.

The craftsmen at the Columban monastery of Kells were influenced by the Scandinavian styles, and although it was alien to their own Irish tradition they

Initial from the Liber Hymnorum, eleventh century

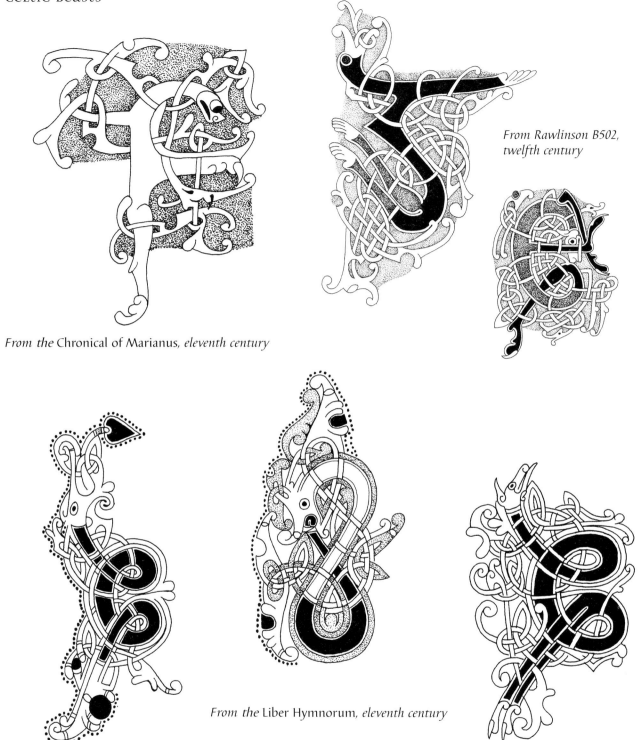

From Rawlinson B502, twelfth century

From the Chronical of Marianus, *eleventh century*

From the Liber Hymnorum, *eleventh century*

soon adapted this new type of ornament competently in their metalwork, such as in the famous Kells Crozier. It also found its way on to the pages of the scribes and the foliage influence can be seen clearly in the eleventh-century *Liber Hymnorum* and the Rawlinson B502 of the twelfth century.

Viking art went through a continuous period of development which lead eventually to the Urnes style, named after a masterpiece of decoration around the doorway of a small church at Urnes, in western Norway. The Urnes influence marked the maturity of the revived art of metalworking in Ireland, its best

Detail from the eleventh-century carved door and portal at Urnes Church, Norway

From the Lismore Crozier, twelfth century

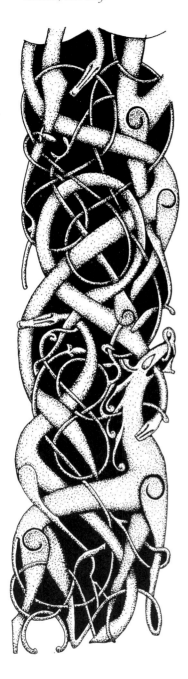

From the shrine of St Lachtin, twelfth century

Above and below:
From the Cross of Cong, twelfth century

known piece being the Cross of Cong, dated by inscription to about 1123, as well as the shrine of St Patrick's Bell and the Lismore and Clonmacnois croziers.

Legend tells us that the twelfth-century *Corpus Missal* was found in an Irish bog, although there is no evidence to prove whether this is fact or legend. Its

twelfth-century scribe introduces the Urnes style of decoration to the initials, with emphasis given to the large ribbon bodies of the beasts in contrast to the thin network of snakes and sinuous lines.

Other books which have similar decoration to the *Corpus Missal* are the *De Consolatione* of Boetius and the *Psalter*. The precise place of origin of these books in Ireland is not known.

From the Cross of Cong, twelfth century

From the Corpus Missal, *twelfth century*

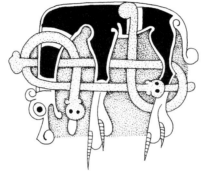

Above and below: From the Corpus Missal, *twelfth century*

From St Patrick's Bell shrine, twelfth century

IRISH DECORATION

THE *BOOK OF KELLS* is called 'The Great Gospel of Columkille, the chief relic of the Western world' in the *Annals of Ulster*. This unique Hiberno-Saxon manuscript displays a rich treasury of densely packed decoration. Like the artistic accomplishment of the Ardagh Chalice, it shows the Irish artists' complete mastery over the medium they chose. The *Book of Kells* was probably started at Iona around 807 CE and then transferred with the relics of Columba to the new monastery at Kells, County Meath, for safety away from the raids of the Vikings.

Man in the jaws of a beast from the Book of Kells, *eighth–ninth century*

Eadfrith's more realistic portrait pages in the *Lind-isfarne Gospels* made a great impression on the other Hiberno-Saxon artists, though none carried on from where he finished as it was a denial of their tradition. The *Book of Kells* portraits reflect a compromise with their unrealistic faces and flat postures and a return to elaborate frameworks of ornamentation. Future books produced at the scriptoria in the ninth century began to be influenced by Viking, Carolingian, English and Continental Romanesque styles and this marked the end of the true Celtic tradition.

From the Book of Kells, *eighth–ninth century*

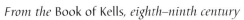

From the Book of Kells, *eighth–ninth century*

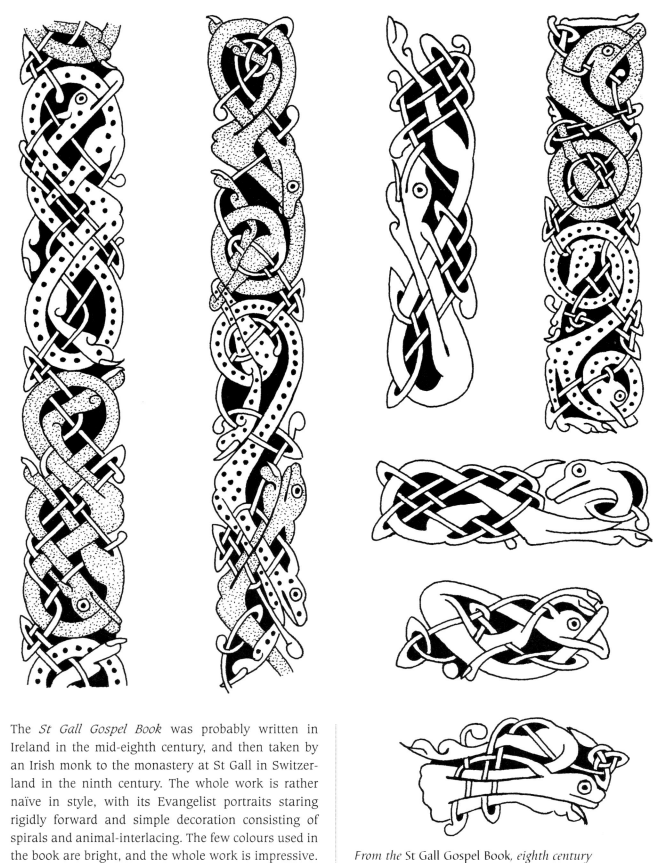

The *St Gall Gospel Book* was probably written in Ireland in the mid-eighth century, and then taken by an Irish monk to the monastery at St Gall in Switzerland in the ninth century. The whole work is rather naïve in style, with its Evangelist portraits staring rigidly forward and simple decoration consisting of spirals and animal-interlacing. The few colours used in the book are bright, and the whole work is impressive.

From the St Gall Gospel Book, *eighth century*

The early ninth-century *Gospel of Mac Regol* is a richly decorated book which is named after its scribe, Mac Regol of Birr (d. 820 CE). Mac Regol was the abbot of the relatively minor monastery at Birr. The artist had no use for a compass, and his work is irregular to the point of recklessness in its improvisation. The ornament consists of interlace, step patterns and animal-interlacing, while the colours are thickly applied.

From the Book of Mac Regol, *early ninth century*

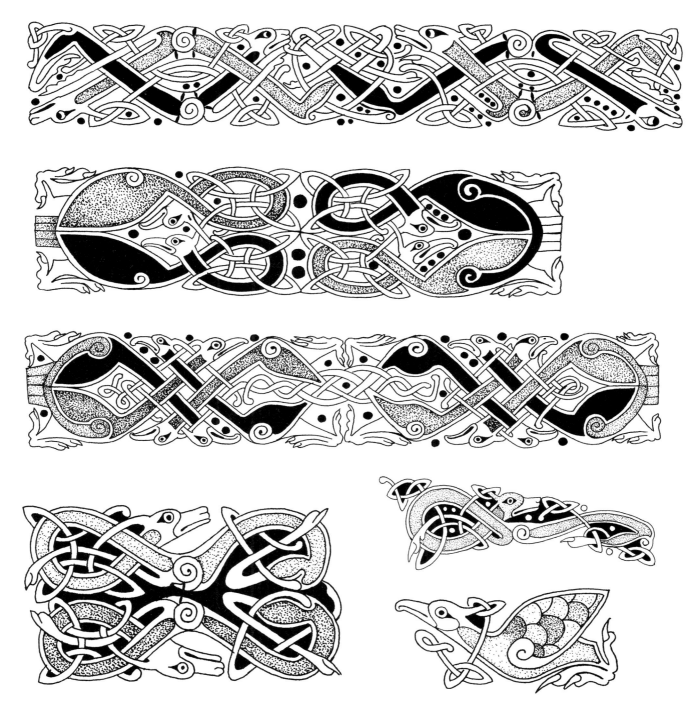

Left: Main panel from the Ricemarcus Psalter, *eleventh century*

Below: Side panels from Ms 40618, late eighth century

Ms 40618 belongs to one of the group of Irish pocket gospels written in the second half of the eighth century. This incomplete gospel book has only one surviving full-page illumination, the portrait of St Luke standing full frontal. This portrait resembles the slightly earlier *Book of Mulling*. The decorative panels either side of saint contain interlaced dogs. This decoration is very weak and looks hurried. It was brought to England in the tenth or eleventh century when it was completed by the scribe Eduardus in the Winchester style.

The *Ricemarcus Psalter* was written by Ithael and Levan who were the sons of Sulien, Bishop of St David's in Wales, around 1079. Sulien (d. 1091) had studied in Ireland and that influence is evident in the initials and decoration.

The Canterbury School

N 596 CE St Augustine, a Benedictine monk landed in England, sent by Pope Gregory, to bring Christianity to the Anglo Saxons. A year later he founded his first abbey, that of St Peter and St Paul at Canterbury, which became a focal point for Christian worship and illumination. All monks had to abide by the rules of St Benedict, which meant that, even for the scribes, a certain amount of time each day had to be set aside for manual work.

From the Canterbury Codex Aureus, *eighth century*

Many manuscripts were written at Canterbury through the centuries. The mid-eighth-century manuscript the *Canterbury Codex Aureus,* is noted for the ancient technique of dyeing the parchment purple, and the use of gold and silver in its decoration. It may have been produced at the expense of King Athelbald of Mercia, whose power extended to Kent at that time. He was known to be a benefactor to Christ Church Cathedral of Canterbury as well as a friend to Cuthbert, Archbishop of Canterbury (d. 758 CE).

CONCLUSION

TWO MAJOR ARCHEOLOGICAL finds in the middle of the nineteenth century not only revealed a great deal about Celtic culture, but, because of the ages of the antiquities recovered, gave their names to the two periods of Celtic history which unfolded during the Iron Age.

Detail from Ms 213, eighth century

The Early Iron Age came to be named after the 1846–62 discoveries on the Austrian Lake Hallstatt, and refers to the period roughly between, the eighth and the fifth centuries BCE – the first phase of Celtic culture. The Late Iron Age, from the fifth century onwards, was named after the 1858 discoveries at the Swiss hamlet of La Tène, adjacent to the village of St Blaise, on the northeast shore of Lake Neuchâtel.

The first Celtic traffic with Britain and Ireland seems to have begun in the La Tène period. This La Tène culture arose in the original Celtic homeland, lying between Switzerland and Hungary, a primary area of devotion to the ancient Bear Mother. Hence we are brought back to where we began, which should be no surprise if we have been thinking like Celts.

The Roman name for Switzerland is Helvetia. Brigantia (Brigid) was a major goddess to the Helvetii, the Celtic forbears of the modern Swiss. The Christian apostle to this area was St Gall (d. 635 CE), one of the many Irish missionaries who came to Europe under the leadership of St Columba (d. 615 CE). St Gall is said to have had a bear companion, who carried his wood for him. This bear is his principal symbol in religious art to this day. His headquarters became the great monastery and town of St Gallen.

East of La Tène is the city of Berne ('She Bear'), southeast of which is Flühli, the birthplace of St Nicholas of Flüh (1417–87), considered by many to be the saviour of the Switzerland. After 20 years of marriage and ten children, on 16 October 1367 at the feast of St Gall, he withdrew from his family and went off to live as a hermit at Ranft. Many people, including some of his older children, thought the action indefensible, unbalanced, immoral, and irresponsible, but he became a spiritual guide whose advice was widely sought and followed. For the rest of his life, he lived only on Holy Communion. His visions led him to the conclusion that he had been given a specific mission in life: to ensure that the Swiss people did not fall apart. When the meeting of the Swiss Confederates on 22 December 1481 at Stans reached a crisis point over the impending civil war, as a last desperate effort to maintain peace they sent a delegate to Nicholas to ask his advice. Nicholas advised the delegate to tell the people to keep the peace in the name of God, and nothing more. But it was enough. On 22 December 1481, without his even being present at the assembly, Nicholas's moral influence was enough to reconcile the dissenting Confederates. He thus averted a civil war, which would probably have been the end of the country, where he is now affectionately remembered as Brother Klaus.

The abrupt shift in the life of Nicholas of Flüh has several shamanic characteristics, among them the apparent onset of imbalance and the withdrawal to the wilderness. He became so popular that his visitors numbered about a hundred a day, and the local priest began to issue permits, just for the sake of order. People usually had to wait two to three weeks to see him. He usually worked until at least midnight, curing all kinds of psychosomatic diseases and giving useful advice to people about their problems. He was clairvoyant and knew what people wanted in advance, usually telling them before they spoke.

He had visions all his life and told one of his confessors that he even remembered having them in his mother's womb. He left records of some of these ecstatic experiences, which include a large number of pagan motifs.

In one of them a heavenly visitor promised that, if he dedicated his life to God, he would receive in heaven a bear's claw and a conqueror's flag as signs of his victory. In lectures she gave to the Jung Institute in 1957 on the subject of these visions, Marie-Louise von Franz pointed out that the bear is a bisexual archetypal symbol which has always been so sacred a creature to the Swiss that, in pre-Christian times, the word 'bear' could not be mentioned, being replaced with euphemisms like 'the old one', 'the holy woman', 'the holy man', 'little grandfather', 'clever father', 'the honey eater', or 'the gold foot' (Marie-Louise Von Franz, 'The Dreams and Visions of St Niklaus von der Flüh' (1957), Lecture 5, pp. 32 and 35.) Carrying such flags with animal symbols was an ancient custom among Nordic shamans and Germanic priests, who also wore long hair and women's clothing.

In another of his visions, Klaus saw a man who came to him as a pilgrim from the place where the sun rises in the summer. The pilgrim sang 'Alleluia' and then begged for alms from Klaus. After receiving it, the pilgrim then took off his hat and Klaus could see that:

> ... he was such a noble, well-built man that he (Klaus) could only look at him with longing and desire. His eyes were black like a magnet, his limbs were so well formed that they were of particular beauty. Although he was dressed, yet his clothes did not prevent his limbs from being seen ... And the Pilgrim's face changed 'like a Veronica' and (Klaus) had a great longing to look at him further ... but his

clothes were changed and he stood before him in trousers and coat with a bearskin over them. The bearskin was sprinkled with golden colour, but he saw and recognised it very well as a bearskin. The bearskin suited him particularly well, so that he the man (Klaus) saw and realised that he (the pilgrim) had a specific beauty .... Then Klaus knew such love for him, that he was quite one with him...

Marie-Louise Von Franz, , 'The Dreams and Visions of St Niklaus von der Flüh' (1957) Lecture 6, p. 42.

Though nothing else in this vision is distinctly Christian, the combination of 'Alleluia' and 'like a Veronica' suggest that Klaus understood the pilgrim to be Christ, though he resembled the old Teutonic god Woden as well. Veronica was the legendary woman who wiped the face of Christ with her veil and then found on it the impression of his face. So the pilgrim in St Nicholas's vision was apparently a handsome, approachable Berserk-Christ.

Just north of St Gallen is the Bodensee, known to the Romans as the Lacus Brigantinus ('Brigid's Lake'), with the city of Bregenz (Roman name 'Brigantia') at the eastern end. Midway across its southern shore is the Swiss hamlet of Kesswil, where, on 26 July 1875, the great psychologist and mystic Carl Gustav Jung was born. One major result of his life's work was to be a reappraisal and appreciation of the often disregarded old divinities and animal totems we have been studying, whom he would now legitimize as being 'archetypal'.

While passing through a wounded and isolated childhood, during which he withdrew into himself and

From the Book of Kells, *eighth–ninth century*

his fantasies, Jung lived in an interior state of deep isolation. When he decided to enter the field of psychology, he found an important father figure in Sigmund Freud, and eventually became Freud's star pupil. But Jung's own gifts and his strong drive towards individuation made it inevitable that he would eventually break with his mentor. The great break, which happened in 1912, was a major trauma for Jung. His whole hard-won outer world collapsed, and he experienced the equivalent of shamanic initiatory sickness or soul loss.

He not only lost faith in Freud at this time but also in the version of Christianity he had received from his father, an orthodox but non-reflective and unimaginative Lutheran pastor. He let go of God's transcendence altogether and declared that God is the libido, the undifferentiated psychic energy, which is present in all of us. On the way to this conclusion, he indulged in all sorts of fantasies peopled by characters like the Teutonic deities Woden and Siegfried. His reflections during this period are full of solar cult imagery:

> The sun is ... really the only rational representation of God, whether we take the point of view of the barbarians of other ages or that of the modern physical sciences ... The sun is adapted as is nothing else to represent the visible God in this world.
>
> Carl Gustav Jung, *Psychology of the Unconscious*, p. 128.

After the publication of *Psychology of the Unconscious*, Jung became a cult figure for many who were involved in contemporary European neo-pagan movements. In his day, there was a resurgence of interest in the Dionysian mysteries. During pre-Lenten revelry, many were known to dress in pagan costume and some even to offer sacrifices to the Great Mother Goddess (Richard Noll, *The Aryan Christ: the Secret Life of Carl Jung*, p. 128). Jung himself was deeply interested in the mysteries surrounding the bull-sacrificing worship of the ancient Iranian solar god Mithras, a deity of correct behaviour and order. The Romans identified Mithras with the Unconquered Sun. Other Mithraic symbols which appear on sculpture are a scorpion, a dog, a raven, and sometimes a lion and a cup with the tip of the sacrificed bull's tail in the form of an ear of grain.

During this liminal period, Jung was often absorbed in non-ordinary reality, hearing voices and having visions. On 12 December 1913, while pondering on his fears, he took a major step: 'Then I let myself drop. Suddenly it was as though the ground literally gave way beneath my feet, and I plunged down into the darkest depths.' (Carl Gustav Jung, *Memories, Dreams, Reflections*, p. 179)

Jung then entered the shamanic Underworld. There he was visited by two ancient spirit guides named Elijah and Salome. Another named Philemon appeared as an old man with a long white beard, bull horns, and kingfisher wings. He opened Jung up to the objectivity of the psyche. Philemon was superseded by yet another named Ka. Soon after this, Jung and his family experienced their house to be dense with the presence of spirits, who all wanted something of Jung. This was not his first encounter with spirits. In 1895, he began attending seances conducted by his cousin, a young medium named Hélène Preiswerk. When he finally begged the spirits in his house to tell him what was going on, their response led to his sitting down and pouring out on paper his 'Seven Sermons of the Dead'. In this document, he set down the essence of his ideas about polar oppositions, masculinity and femininity, and the relation of sexuality to spirit. After this, the spirits stopped bothering his household; and Jung was launched into his new life as a wounded healer. In 1916 he finally legitimized the lessons he had learned from the seances and the apparitions with the term 'active imagination'.

During a lecture, Jung once used a large coloured diagram to illustrate the layers of the human unconscious. He coloured the lowest level red and called it the 'central fire', making it sound very much like the Kundalini energy which runs up the spine through the chakras. The next to the lowest layer he called the layer of animal ancestry, which he believed was present in every human psyche, and above that was the layer of primeval ancestors. (Smith, C. Michael, *Jung and Shamanism in Dialogue*, p. 105.) On another occasion, referring to our animal ancestry, he asserted that there is a bear with glowing eyes deep 'in the human unconscious'. (Shephard, Paul, and Sanders, Barry, *The Sacred Paw*, pp. xiii-xiv.)

Jung identified several other layers of an individual's unconscious, but the animal level is the one of particular interest to the subject of this book. While Jung's personal helpers were either human or quasi-human spirit guides, rather than totem animals, in his visionary experiences of December 1913, he saw 'himself as a crucified Christ, who then assumed the form of a lion-headed god'. (Richard Noll, *The Aryan Christ*, p. 138.)

Further contributions which Jung made to psychology are in new understandings of the nature of complexes, the notions of anima and animus, the pattern of a self's individuation and the significance of archetypes, which Jung considered to be the functional units of which the collective unconscious is composed. He described archetypes as 'the identical psychic structures common to all', which together continue 'the archaic heritage of humanity'. (quoted in Anthony Stevens, *Jung*, p. 33)

Jung's realization that, in addition to having an individual unconscious, each of us share in a 'collective unconscious', was itself another breakthrough. He considered the collective unconscious to be: '... the source of the imagery which rises to the surface in cultural myth and ritual, which informs and structures religious and moral ideation, and which provides the ideological ground of sociocultural ordering.' (Smith, C. Michael, *Jung and Shamanism in Dialogue*, p. 105)

From this collective unconscious have emerged all the animal symbols and the anthropomorphized divinities we have considered in this book. While most branches of Christianity have long tended either to demonize or to regard scornfully pre-Christian religion – and some have transferred this attitude to whatever they choose to label 'New Age' – Jung's extraordinary contribution to the field of psychology has helped many sensible people to appreciate the vital necessity of understanding these archetypes because of all they can teach us about ourselves. Brigid, who was goddess of healing and therapy, would probably be very pleased with this development.

The bearded wine god Silenos in a feline form

Above and below: From Durham Cassiodorus, *eighth century*

You can view the art of Courtney Davis on his web site:

www.celtic-art.com

Bibliography

Ashe, Geoffrey, *Dawn Behind the Dawn* (Henry Holt, New York, 1992)

Baring, Anne, and Cashford, Jules, *The Myth of the Goddess* (Arkana, New York, 1991)

Baring-Gould, S., and Fisher, J., ed. Bryce, Derek, *Lives of the British Saints* (Llanerch Enterprises, Llanerch, 1990)

Benedictine Monks of St Augustine's Abbey, Ramsgate, *The Book of Saints* (Morehouse Publishing, Harrisburg, PA, 1989)

Begg, Ean, *The Cult of the Black Virgin* (Arkana, New York, 1985)

Bonwick, James, *Irish Druids and Old Irish Religions* (Dorset Press, Dorset, 1986)

Berger, Pamela, *The Goddess Obscured* (Beacon Press, Boston, 1985)

Bitel, Lisa M., *Land of Women* (Cornell University Press, Ithaca and London, 1996)

Bord, Janet and Colin, *Sacred Waters* (Granada, New York, 1985)

Brenneman, Walter L., Jr., and Mary G., *Crossing the Circle at the Holy Wells of Ireland* (University of Virginia Press, Charlottesville, VA, 1995)

Condren, Mary, *The Serpent and the Goddess* (Harper San Francisco, San Francisco, 1989)

Cowaki, Tom, *Fire in the Head* (Harper San Francisco, San Francisco, 1993)

Cunliffe, Barry, *The Celtic World* (McGraw-Hill Book Company, New York, 1979)

Dames, Michael, *Mythic Ireland* (Thames & Hudson, London, 1992)

D'Arcy, Mary Ryan, *The Saints of Ireland* (The Irish American Cultural Institute, St Paul MM, 1974)

Davidson, Hilda Ellis, *The Lost Beliefs of Northern Europe* (Routledge, New York, 1993)

DePaor, Liam, *Saint Patrick's World* (University of Notre Dame Press, Notre Dame, 1993)

Douglas, Adam, *The Beast Within* (Orion, London, 1992)

Ellis, Peter Berresford, *The Druids* (William B. Eerdmans Publishing Company, Grand Rapids, Michigan, 1994)

Farrar, Janet and Stewart, *The Witches' Goddess* (Phoenix Publishing Inc., Custer, Washington, 1987)

Frazer, Sir James G., *The Golden Bough* (The Macmillan Company, New York, 1960)

Gerald of Wales, *The History and Topography of Ireland* (Penguin Books, New York, 1982)

Gimbutas, Marija, *The Civilization of the Goddess* (Harper San Francisco, San Francisco, 1991)

Gimbutas, Marija, *The Language of the Goddess* (Harper San Francisco, San Francisco, 1991)

Goodrich, Norrfta Lorre, *Merlin* (Harper Perennial, New York, 1988)

Graves, Robert, *The White Goddess* (Farrar, Strauss and Giroux, New York, 1993)

Gregory, Lady Augusta, *A Book of Saints and Wonders* (Colin Smythe Limited, Gerrards Cross, Buckinghamshire, 1993)

Griffen, Toby D., *Names From the Dawn of British Legend* (Llanerch Publishers, Felinfach, 1994)

Harrison, Michael, *The London that Was Rome* (George Allen and Unwin Ltd., London, 1971)

Henderson, George, *From Durrow to Kells*, (Thames & Hudson, London, 1987)

Henken, Elissa R., *Traditions of the Welsh Saints* (D.S. Brewer, Wolfeboro, NH, 1987)

Hera, Gerhard, *The Celts* (Barnes & Noble, New York, 1976)

Hutton, Ronald, *The Pagan Religions of the Ancient British Isles* (Blackwell, Oxford, 1991)

Hutton, Ronald, *The Stations of the Sun* (Oxford University Press, Oxford, 1996)

Ivanits, Linda J., *Russian Folk Beliefs* (M.E. Sharpe Inc., Armonk, NY, 1989)

Jaraal, Michele, *Deerdancer* (Arkana, New York, 1995)

Johnson, Buffie, *Lady of the Beasts* (Harper & Row, San Francisco, 1981)

Jones, Kathy, *The Ancient British Goddess* (Ariadne Publications, Glastonbury, 1991)

Jones, Prudence, and Pennick, Nigel, *A History of Pagan Europe* (Routledge, London, 1995)

Jung, Carl Gustav, trans. Hinkle, Beatrice, *Psychology of the Unconscious: A Study of the Transformations and Symbolisms of the Libido*, (Moffat Yard, New York, 1916)

Jung, Carl Gustav, *Memories, Dreams Reflections,* revised edition ed. Aniela Jaffe (Pantheon Books, New York, 1962)

Knightly, Charles, *The Customs and Ceremonies of Britain* (Thames & Hudson, London, 1986)

Laing, Lloyd and Jenny, *The Picts and the Scots* (Alan Sutton, Dover, NH, 1993)

MacCana, Proinsias, *Celtic Mythology* (Peter Bedrick Books, New York, 1983)

Mann, Nicholas R., *The Keltic Power Symbols* (Triskele, Glastonbury, 1987)

Markale, Jean, *The Celts* (Inner Traditions, Rochester, VT, 1993)

—— *Merlin* (Inner Traditions, Rochester, VT, 1995)

—— *Women of the Celts* (Inner Traditions, Rochester, VT, 1975)

Matthews, Caitlin and John, *The Encyclopedia of Celtic Wisdom* (Barnes & Noble, New York, 1994)

The Aquarian Guide to British & Irish Mythology (The Aquarian Press, Northamptonshire, 1988)

Matthews, John, and Potter, Chesca, *The Aquarian Guide to Legendary London* (The Aquarian Press, Northamptonshire, 1990)

Matthews, John, *The Celtic Shaman* (Element, Rockport, Massachusetts, 1992)

—— *Taliesin* (The Aquarian Press, London, 1991)

MacCulloch, J.A., *The Religion of the Ancient Celts* (Studio Editions, London, 1992)

MacNeill, Maire, *The Festival of Lughnasa* (Oxford University Press, Oxford, 1962)

McLean, Adam, *The Triple Goddess* (Phanes Press, Grand Rapids, Michigan, 1989)

McNeill, F. Marian, *The Silver Bough* (Canongate Publishing, Edinburgh, 1989)

Moore, Robert, and Gilette, Douglas, *The Magician Within* (William Morrow and Company Inc., New York, 1993)

Noll, Richard, *The Aryan Christ* (Random House, New York, 1997)

O'Brien, Maire Cruise, 'The Role of the Poet in Gaelic Society', *The Celtic Continuum* (George Braziller, New York, 1982)

O'Driscoll, Robert, ed., *The Celtic Consciousness* (George Braziller, New York, 1981)

Pennick, Nigel, *Celtic Sacred Landscapes* (Thames & Hudson, London, 1996)

Phillips, Graham, *The Search for the Graill* (Century, London, 1995)

Phillips, Guy Ragland, *Brigantiall* (Routledge & Kegan Paul, London, 1976)

Rankin, H. D., *Celts and the Classical World* (Areopagitica Press, London & Sydney, 1987)

Rolleston, T. W., *Celtic* (Senate, London, 1994)

Ross, Anne, *Folklore of the Scottish Highlands* (Barnes & Noble, New York, 1976)

Ross, Anne, *Pagan Celtic Britain* (Constable, London, 1992)

Roy, James Charles, *Islands of Storm* (Dufour Editions Inc., Chester Springs, Pennsylvania, 1991)

Rutherford, Walter, *Celtic Lore* (The Aquarian Press, London, 1993)

Schmitt, Jean-Claude, *The Holy Greyhound* (Cambridge University Press, Cambridge, 1983)

Seignolle, Claude et Jacques, 'Le Folklore du Hurepoix' (in Van Gennep, Arnold, *Manuel du Folklore Français*, Paris, 1943–58)

Shepard, Paul, and Sanders, Barry, *The Sacred Paw* (Arkana, New York, 1985)

Smith, C. Michael, *Jung and Shamanism in Dialogue* (Paulist Press, New York, 1997)

Spence, Lewis, *The Mysteries of Britain* (Blacken Books, London, 1993)

Stewart, R. J., *Celtic Gods, Celtic Goddesses* (Blandford, London, 1990)

Stewart, R. J., *Merlin and Woman* (Blandford, New York, 1988)

Stewart, R. J., *Waters of the Gap* (Ashgrove Press, Bath, 1989)

Stevens, Anthony, *Jung* (Oxford University Press, Oxford, 1994)

Tolstoy, Nikolai, *The Quest for Merlin* (Little, Brown and Company, Boston, 1985)

Toulson, Shirley, *The Celtic Year* (Element, Rockport, MA, 1993)

Towill, Edwin Sprott, *Saints of Scotland* (Saint Andrew Press, Edinburgh, 1994)

Van Gennep, Arnold, 'Le folklore de la Bourgogne (Côte d'Or)' (in *Manuel du Folklore Français*, Paris, 1944–58)

Von Franz, Marie-Louise, transcript of a series of nine lectures she delivered on 'The Dreams and Visions of St Niklaus von der Flüh', delivered to the Jung Institute, 8 May–10 July, 1957

Walker, Barbara G., *The Woman's Encyclopedia of Myths and Secrets* (Harper San Francisco, San Francisco, 1983)

Webster, Graham, *Celtic Religion in Roman Britain* (Barnes & Noble, Totowa, NJ, 1987)

Illustrations pp.1-7

p. 1 Cernunnos, lord of the animals

p. 2 Eighth-century Irish crozier head in bronze with glass and enamel

p. 3 The lion, symbol of St Mark, from the seventh-century *Echternach Gospels*;
Border from the *Book of Kells*, eighth–ninth century

p. 4 Adapted border from the *Book of Kells*, eighth–ninth century

p. 5 Adapted border from the Book of Kells, eighth–ninth century

p. 6 Eighth-century border from Ms 213, Cologne;
Irish-style decorative mount with eagle heads in copper alloy

p. 7 Adapted design from the *Durham Gospels,* seventh–eighth century;
Border from the *Lindisfarne Gospels,* seventh–eighth century

Index